CH00433872

Best wishes

Anthony Seely.

AGILE
MARKETING

HOW TO INNOVATE FASTER, CHEAPER AND WITH LOWER RISK

ANTHONY FREELING

Published by Goldingtons Press.

978-1456491093 (U.S. Paperback)
978-0956780904 (Hardback)
978-0956780911 (U.K. Paperback)

Library of Congress Control Number: 2010919420

For Laurel, Matthew and Catharine

CONTENTS

ACKNOWLEDGMENTS

This book has been over 10 years in the development. My interest in how companies can become more customer-centric arose from my consulting work while a Partner at McKinsey & Company. As Leader of the Marketing Practice in Europe, I was involved in a series of "Commercial Transformation" studies with leading businesses in a variety of industries: fast moving consumer goods, retailing, medical devices, marketing services and technology. We had a clear point of view on what good marketing was and were successful in applying these ideas to our clients.

However, with the benefit of hindsight, I realized that some of these businesses, after strong initial improvements, were unable to maintain excellent marketing and sales performance. I have always been passionate about my work having impact and it was frustrating to see my former clients doing poor marketing in spite of all our efforts. Furthermore, some of these businesses failed to adapt to the challenges of the new millennium and were taken over, shrunken in scale, or otherwise subject to the rigors of Creative Destruction.

With the support of my Partners, I began an internal research project into Commercial Transformation – how could McKinsey help clients permanently transform their commercial capabilities and be truly customer-centric. Particular mention for their support should go to my fellow leaders of the Marketing and of the Consumer Practices: Trond Riiber Knudsen, Hajo Riesenbeck, Peter Freedman, Thomas Tochtermann and David Court.

On retiring from McKinsey I felt the job remained incomplete and so I joined the Ashridge Strategic Management Centre (ASMC), which has both afforded me the freedom to pursue the topic in a more academic environment and provided challenge to my evolving thoughts at every turn. Marcus Alexander, Felix Barber, Andrew Campbell, Michael Goold and Jo Whitehead each helped me develop and refine the logic of this book in a series of challenging, and usually stimulating, meetings.

Thanks also to all the member companies of ASMC who added their own experience and thoughts to enrich the content. Special mention is due to Stephen Bungay who not only took part in those meetings but also read every chapter of this book in various draft forms, giving unfailingly helpful advice. His ideas come from a very different starting point to mine, but our thoughts on feedback loops between execution and decision have coincided and indeed I have borrowed directly from his work on Execution in Chapters 9 and 10.

I benefited also from the experience of many former McKinsey colleagues, now in the business world, who had been through the client work with me. They gave generously of their time in providing evidence to support or disprove my ideas over the past few years. These include, in particular, Carolyn Hunter, Frazer Smith, Helen Buck, Sue Whalley and William Eccleshare.

Finally, my heartfelt thanks and love to my wife, Laurel Powers-Freeling, who not only had to put up with the inevitable ups and downs along the way, but also provided several specific case studies that are used in the book and proofread the entire manuscript.

All of these people have provided advice and support, without which this book would probably never have come to fruition. Of course, this book is not perfect. Any errors, weaknesses in argument and clumsiness of communication are my responsibility. I hope that, in spite of that, you will be able to understand and find useful the ideas it contains.

INTRODUCTION

On 13 February 1995, Tesco, one of the largest UK supermarket chains, launched a customer loyalty program called Clubcard. On 23 October 1995, Safeway, one of Tesco's main rivals, launched its own program, named the ABC card.

Both programs offered customers a 1% discount, and might therefore have been expected to result in greater loyalty and correspondingly increased sales. But that was not why either Tesco or Safeway launched their programs. For both of them, the real opportunity lay in using the data provided by the cards. These cards enabled them for the first time to link sales to individual customers. Rather than simply deriving aggregate data from till receipts, the cards would allow them to learn what a particular individual had done on previous store visits, and so build up a picture of each customer's shopping patterns. The 1% discount was the price the companies paid to their customers for information about them.

The Clubcard and ABC programs led to very different results.

Emboldened by initial successes that reaffirmed the value of the new data, Safeway sought to analyze every element of every transaction. In attempting to develop a deep understanding of its customers, it adopted a segmentation approach capturing all the intricacies of shopper behavior. This enormous analytical undertaking failed to result in any real insights or value creating actions.

Tesco, on the other hand, began by throwing away most of the data in an attempt to develop a few useful insights. When these insights were proven to be of value, Tesco slowly added complexity to its analyses and to the activities they prompted. Every year, the complexity grew and the number of activities multiplied.

In 2004, Safeway was sold to its smaller UK competitor Morrison's. At the time of writing, Clubcard is the largest loyalty card in the UK and

Tesco has almost twice the market share of its nearest rival, making it the third largest retailer in the world.

Why were the results of such similar enterprises so radically different?

Tesco did not know more than Safeway when it launched its card – though it did know a lot more in the end. Nor did it collect better data – though the data it ended up with was far more valuable. Nor did it have better IT systems – though ABC overloaded Safeway's systems.

I suggest that Tesco succeeded and Safeway failed because they had a radically different approach to marketing. The approach adopted by Tesco poses a fundamental challenge to deep-seated assumptions held in marketing departments throughout the world. I call it 'Agile Marketing' and I will argue that for many companies adopting it has become a matter of survival.

CHAPTER I

THE BROKEN PROMISE OF MARKETING

Marketing has been around in some form for a very long time, but only over the past hundred years has it emerged as a specialist discipline in its own right. It has attracted large budgets in many industries, starting in consumer goods manufacturing but moving over time into retailing, automotive, telephony, pharmaceuticals, financial services and public services.

Marketing has promised much, but many feel it has broken its promises. Why?

A BIG PROMISE?

If Economics is the dismal science, Marketing is the optimistic function. Certainly, its proponents see it as the way to achieve a myriad of goals. Peter Drucker claimed that together with innovation (which many marketers anyway see as a subset of marketing) it is one of only two basic functions, with all the rest being costs. A recent book by Nirmalya Kumar (2004, p. 2),[1] a Professor at London Business School, proclaims that marketing can, and indeed must, "help CEO's lead organization-wide transformational initiatives that deliver substantial revenue growth and increased profitability." A book co-authored by John Quelch, the Senior Associate Dean at Harvard Business School, proposes marketing to be "more democratic than politics" in making the case that marketing should both provide a lesson to democracy and can be used to strengthen democracy (Quelch and Jocz, 2008, Front Flap).[2]

Practitioners too are bullish, for example Mark Sherrington (2003, p. xiii),[3] a former consultant and Chief Marketing Officer of one of the world's largest drinks companies wrote in his book, "Companies are addicted to growth – and like the worst addict they will do whatever it takes to get it. ... time has shown that marketing is the surest fix of all."

The most famous textbook on marketing management, (Kotler, 1991, p. 4)[4] taught to generations of MBA students, states, "We believe that stronger company marketing skills can potentially launch a new era of high economic growth and rising living standards."

This positive view of marketing is by no means restricted to the written word. In recent years the rhetoric has been matched by actions. Marketing budgets have outstripped inflation. Traditional marketers have over the past decade been launching programs to build their marketing capabilities. Global brand leaders such as Coca-Cola, Gillette, Unilever and Diageo have each committed major resources to these efforts.

At the same time businesses that have never embraced marketing are launching major change programs aimed at getting closer to customers, often under the heading of "customer centricity". Examples include life assurance companies, energy utilities, pharmaceutical companies, engineering and other B2B organizations. These new industries have created marketing departments and spent money on advertising, direct mail and Customer Relationship Management (CRM) systems.

For example, while traditional big spenders such as Procter & Gamble and Unilever were in the top 10 advertisers in the UK in 2009,[5] The Government's Central Office of Information (COI) was number 1 with over £200m of advertising spend; Satellite TV broadcaster BSkyB was fourth; retailers Tesco, Asda and DFS were all in the top 10. The rest of the top 30 was filled with five telephone companies, retailers, and packaged goods companies as well as car manufacturers, while lower down were banks, insurance companies, drug makers and energy companies. These numbers exclude the direct marketing spends, which are dominated by the financial companies.

With such potential to transform businesses, the economy and society, and so much money going towards the objectives surely nothing can stand in the way of marketing to fulfilling its promise.

PROMISE UNFULFILLED

However something is not right. As long ago as 1993 my colleagues at McKinsey and I were writing that, "doubts are surfacing about the very basis of contemporary marketing: the value of ever more costly brand advertising, which often dwells on seemingly irrelevant points of difference; of promotions, which are often just a fancy name for price cutting; and of large marketing departments, which, far from being an asset, are often a millstone around an organization's neck."[6] Today there is continuing disenchantment with the function of marketing (despite some successes) on the part of customers, business leaders and indeed the marketing community itself.

Even though marketers claim to understand customer needs and tailor products or services that meet those needs, customers are not noticeably more satisfied than they were 15 years ago. In a recent book, Paddy Barwise of London Business School and Sean Meehan of IMD observed that customers' levels of satisfaction across many sectors have not improved over the past decade and more.[7] For example, the American Customer Satisfaction Index (ACSI) only reached 75.0 in Q3, 2008 having been at 74.8 when it was started in summer of 1994. Barwise and Meehan suggest this has to do with too much focus on being different and not enough on meeting the basic requirements demanded by customers in the market place.

Business leaders, who have after all funded the expansion in budgets, nevertheless have a surprisingly mixed opinion of marketing. Not only are marketers the butt of jokes around the Board table – How many Marketing Directors does it take to change a light bulb? Don't worry, we'll just say the darkness is a feature – but the concerns continue in serious conversation. For example, in a survey I led for the Marketing Society in 2005 marketing departments were described by their own CEO's as creative, committed, hard working, inspiring, essential, passionate and talented, yet at the same time considered to be undisciplined, not value-orientated, inconsistent, self-important, not commercial, narrow, and not accountable. This is a similar finding to other surveys that have been carried out, both qualitative and quantitative, over the past few years.

Two particular gripes emerge from discussions with CEO's. First, senior management is always looking for greater efficiency and returns from marketing, yet often feels this imperative is falling on deaf ears. As Philip Kotler wrote in 2004, CEO's are "growing impatient with marketing. They feel that they get accountability for their investments in finance, production, information technology, even purchasing, but don't know what their marketing spending is achieving."[8] Second, CEO's have consistently been frustrated both by the lack of game-changing innovations from their marketing departments and by being blindsided by competitors who do seem to come up with these innovations.

Given these concerns, it is perhaps unsurprising that in the recent downturn, and in every other recession in recent memory, the marketing budget has been amongst the first to be cut, in spite of an ongoing argument from the marketing community that this is an investment that will more than pay for itself when the upturn comes. Marketers also feel that too often the operational management of their businesses let them down through poor execution of the plans developed by their marketing departments.

One type of initiative that was tried by several companies over the past few years has been to centralize marketing under the leadership of a "Chief Marketing Officer" (CMO). The goal in most cases was to develop a Center of Excellence that would be able to build capabilities in marketing across the organization, as well as to be guardian of the corporate brand. This seemingly positive step, of bringing marketing into the top management team of the company, has been far from successful.

For example, in 2004 Spencer Stuart, the headhunters, wrote a pamphlet arguing that CMO's had the riskiest jobs in America, with an average tenure below 2 years and in some industries below one year. This trend has continued, with stories about CMO's retiring to "pursue other opportunities" in the marketing trade press almost every week. A recent academic paper found that "the presence of a CMO has no impact on firm performance",[9] which may explain their short tenure.

In fact, the marketing community itself continues to exhibit many signs of depression. Donald Lehmann, Executive Director of the Marketing Science Institute, a leading marketing think tank, stated in preparation for a seminar on Excellence in Marketing, "Marketing as a function is in some danger of being marginalized".[10] The Marketing Society, the industry body in Great Britain, observed that the average tenure of marketing leaders is less than 2 years and was moved to issue a "Manifesto for Marketing" in 2005 as an attempt to reinvigorate the role of marketing in UK business. For an optimistic profession, marketing does seem to be pretty down on itself.

One reason for this may be the problems faced by companies that have invested in building marketing capabilities and becoming customer centric. These are not small initiatives – typically they involve organization restructuring, extensive training, hiring and firing and pilot projects rolled out across countries and business units. They can last for years and cost many millions. This scale of change programs is great for the consulting industry, but is it good for shareholders and for customers? At best the jury is out on that. In my own consulting experience I worked with several companies on these issues, but with mixed success. In some cases the changes we identified were successful in the market place and were still in place 10 or more years later. But in other cases initial enthusiasm waned and the companies largely reverted to type over the following few years. In my more recent experience with Executive Education, I note that the customer centric change business is still relatively buoyant but the support from the CEO and other functions appears to be waning. Perhaps this will prove to be just another fad – but how can we square that with the high aspirations of the Promised Land?

THE BIG QUESTION

I have painted a picture of promise unfulfilled. Consequently, I believe that the big question facing marketing today is:

How must marketing change to achieve its promise?

When I first started to research this book, my belief was that the problem was largely organizational. I felt that "good marketing" was quite well understood by the best businesses as well as by consultants (including, of course, me) and indeed that we already had the blueprint for marketing excellence. Based upon the principles of customer insight, segmentation, positioning and measurement, it had been proven over and over again to provide growth and return on marketing investment. However (I thought) most companies were struggling to execute against the blueprint due to a combination of organizational culture and capabilities. Therefore I saw the challenge as refining the approach taken in change programs, to reflect the unique nature of marketing capabilities as opposed to other forms of operational skills.

As my work progressed, however, I increasingly found the need to challenge this assumption. I found that my model of excellent marketing did not reflect the way the best marketers actually worked – or at least not how they worked most of the time. I realized that some of the lessons from economics and other fields of work suggested that a more agile, adaptive and intuitive approach to marketing could help marketing achieve its promise. In particular, in the bicentenary of Charles Darwin's birth, I found that the theory of natural selection in evolution could be applied to marketing offers as the basis of a new theory of marketing.

At the same time, my previous beliefs about good marketing were not entirely wrong – at times a more rational, measured approach undoubtedly worked. Therefore I needed to arrive at a synthesis of these two apparently opposite approaches before I could be satisfied that I was answering the Big Question. In this book, I provide my synthesis.

SHAPE, ADAPT AND COMPETE BEFORE YOU LEAP

This book argues that the current approaches to marketing are largely based on making big leaps.

Whenever marketers gather, there is an ongoing demand for, and fascination with, major marketing strategy changes. Innovation is the new black; the media delights in documenting successful companies that have transformed their fortunes with great new marketing. Apple and Google are examples of large companies viewed as marketing successes; smaller ones include, in the UK, Innocent Drinks, Green & Blacks chocolate and The Number (118 118).

But do these undoubtedly successful examples demonstrate that breakthrough marketing innovation is always a good idea? We know that the vast majority of new products on grocery shelves fail. We know that for every "great marketing success story" there are many more examples of "marketing failures".

In fact, I am unconvinced that we know whether the successes are due to best practice, or simply the result of a "marketing lottery" whereby a few initiatives win while the majority lose. And even if they succeed initially, do they continue to win? Or is the initial spurt of success soon overtaken by competitors moving more steadily, as with Tesco?

My argument is that aiming at this sort of big leap is often the wrong objective. It assumes a level of knowledge about the future and about the reactions of customers and competitors far greater than is realistic. Instead, most of the time marketing should be seeking to adapt to the surprises of the marketplace in as agile a way as possible. This is best done through small incremental changes, not big leaps.

This drive towards incremental change has taken root in other functional areas. Continuous improvement has become the mantra in manufacturing, logistics and procurement. It is taken as a given that good companies continually reduce costs and that this is a major plank of successful strategies. Management philosophies and tools such as Lean Manufacturing, Just-in-time, and Six Sigma have all been developed to enable this. Yet there has been no such trend in marketing. Managers might assume that their products or services will keep on improving, or that their marketing activities will become ever more effective – but how? What process will deliver continuous improvement in marketing?

In biology, the theory of evolution through natural selection addresses incremental change. Darwin's "dangerous idea" has over the past 150 years developed not only in biology but has been increasingly applied to other disciplines, including economics. Evolution describes how organisms adapt to their environment through survival of the fittest. To my knowledge it has not been used in marketing. I shall show how the theory can be applied.

Natural selection, at its most basic, is an iterative process of **variation**, **selection** and **replication**: from a parent organism different variations are created, these variations compete for resources and survival in the environment and some are selected to survive (the fittest), and the winners then replicate to create a new generation of variants. Each of these steps is critical – variation to allow change in the population, selection to ensure the adapted organisms survive and replication to ensure there are more of the winning variants in the next generation. Over time, the population evolves.

Similarly, when marketing offers are viewed as offers fighting for resources in a competitive landscape, we can define a process of natural selection. By implementing an approach to Test, Learn and Commit (TLC), marketers can create offers that are adapted to their own competitive landscape and that will change over time as that landscape changes. I will show how this can be achieved through a combination of Test-and-Learn loops with the operational capability to commit resources to the successful trials.

This is Agile Marketing.

It is important to note that Agile Marketing is not just for making small changes. Biological evolution showed that creatures that people previously believed must have been created through divine intervention could in fact evolve through natural selection. Similarly, while individual changes may be relatively small, over time Agile Marketing can achieve breakthroughs previously believed only to be achievable through big leaps. By adapting to the environment fast enough, an offer can actually shape the marketplace in its own favor. Previously winning competing offers will no longer be well adapted.

SUMMARY OF THE BOOK

Part 1: Why has marketing failed to live up to its promise?

In the first part of this book, I examine why marketing has failed to live up to its promise and I provide a new definition of marketing that makes clearer what it is trying to achieve; I introduce the concepts of Agile Marketing and fast Test, Learn and Commit Loops, and discuss how to make them work. In this part I focus on the most prevalent form of Agile Marketing – Evolutionary Marketing.

In Chapter 2, I examine how the promise of marketing has been articulated and why it is not being fulfilled. First, I look at the definitions of marketing according to marketers. If marketing academics and writers are to be believed, marketing has become required for companies to succeed. Yet there is no commonly agreed definition of what it is; and the most current definitions do little to reduce possible confusion.

More worryingly, other functions do not seem to accept the definitions of marketing that marketers themselves believe. What marketers call marketing, most people call strategy, which is a pretty fundamental mismatch.

I explain how this has happened as a result of the history of marketing and its development, examining three distinct eras. I then propose my own definition of marketing; this should help readers be clear as to what I am talking about and also move forward the general discussion of "what is marketing?" My definition is:

> *Marketing is the process of creating and communicating winning offers that profitably attract customer spend in an uncertain market environment. It does this by:*
> - *Shaping the market environment through innovation*
> - *Adapting to changes in the environment, and*
> - *Beating competition.*

This definition brings out the importance of the market context and the importance of adapting to it and seeking to shape it. It also talks explicitly about beating competition, unlike many such definitions.

In Chapter 3, I discuss the changes, challenges and tensions at the heart of marketing meeting its goals. At the same time as there is disappointment with the historical progress achieved by marketing and even as doubts are beginning to be raised about major change initiatives, the world in which marketers work is becoming more challenging.

There is a rapidly changing environment with proliferating complexity: proliferation of customer segments, of sales and service channels and communication media and of stakeholders including shareholders, government and regulators and local communities. Businesses have globalized, exposing them to a wider variety of cultures, distribution networks and customer demands. On top of all that there is the increased speed of change.

In short, marketers today need to create, deliver and communicate better offers to their customers more rapidly than ever before and as efficiently as possible.

There are therefore three marketing challenges to be met simultaneously:

- **Fitness.** Meeting customer needs and other stakeholder demands...
- **Speed.** ...Delivered before competition...
- **Efficiency.** ...At a lower cost

These three challenges must be met, yet they seem to be in conflict. To be fit sounds expensive and time consuming, speed risks being quick and dirty, while efficiency seems to suggest a cost-cutting mentality, as opposed to seeking creativity to achieve growth.

There is also an ongoing tension between intuition and rigor in marketing that has served to block some of the approaches that businesses have followed to improve marketing.

I argue that some of the problems that marketing faces have arisen because the genuine challenges created by these tensions have not been grasped. In other functions, continuous improvement has been a key part of the answer to coping with the need for fitness, speed and efficiency in a rapidly changing environment. To date, the lack of a continuous improvement approach to marketing is the main gap in marketing theory. That gap is what my theory of Agile Marketing seeks to close.

Part 2: Evolutionary Marketing and Test, Learn, Commit Loops

Darwin used the shorthand "survival of the fittest" to summarize his theory of natural selection. I argue that marketing too is seeking to find the fittest offers that will survive not in the jungle, but in the marketplace. I clarify in this book that "fitness" in the marketing context means that the offer not only attracts customer demand but also meets other stakeholder requirements.

I first look briefly at the basics of the theories of evolution and natural selection. I show that the essence of natural selection in biology is a continuous process of variation, selection and replication. It is also an essentially competitive theory with winners and losers in a battle for scarce resources. Fitness in biology is always defined relative to the environment in which a creature lives – its ability to survive and reproduce.

I then discuss the relatively recent application of the theory of evolution to economics. This attempts to describe evolutionary activity as the result of different institutions competing to survive and grow in an economic landscape, doing what it takes. Evolutionary economics is a theory of constant change in a world of imperfect human beings, in contrast to more traditional economic theory that assumes a move towards steady-state equilibrium of theoretically perfectly decision makers. Both the dynamism and human fallibility are features of the marketing world.

Therefore, I suggest that the same evolutionary ideas can be applied to marketing offers. I propose that fitness in marketing relates to the market environment in which an offer competes. Evolutionary theorists have used the idea of searching a fitness landscape to explain how natural selection works. I adapt this analogy to describe how marketing can be thought of as a search on a marketing landscape. Trying to find the best marketing offer means trying to find the fittest place on the landscape.

The current textbook approach to marketing is to perform market research, develop insights into customer needs, and then to create offers that meet those needs. In fitness landscape terms, this means trying to understand the landscape and to make a big leap to the fittest point. But the problem with the big leap approach is that we don't really know if an offer is fit before the offer is actually made. All the evidence is that these big leaps are very risky: most new products fail.

The theory of natural selection suggests an alternative way to search for fitness – through a large number of small steps each of which makes a small improvement to fitness. These small steps can be achieved through executing Test, Learn and Commit (TLC) loops. By trying out lots of tests, learning which are more successful, and then committing to these successes, marketers can allow their marketing offers to evolve to be the fittest in the marketplace. I call this approach Evolutionary Marketing. It is the most common form of Agile Marketing (Figure 1-1).

This is a way of applying the ideas of continuous improvement, so common in other functions, to marketing. TLC loops enable simultaneous improvement of fitness, speed and efficiency.

The remainder of chapter 4 examines each of the steps of Test, Learn and Commit in more detail.

In Chapter 5, I look at two case studies: Tesco, the U.K. based retailer and Capital One, the U.S. based credit card company.

How to conduct Agile Marketing: Test, Learn, Commit (TLC) loops

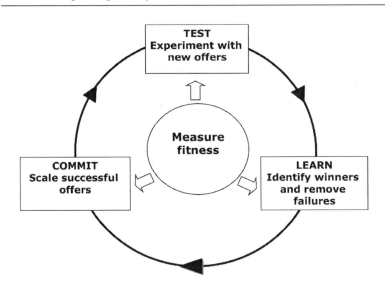

Figure 1-1

Part 3: Making it work

Biological evolution is not a perfect analogy to marketing, due in particular to the fact that marketers can make choices, whereas biological evolution assumes randomness. Can we improve on random Test-and-Learn loops? When seeking to develop the capability to become an Agile Marketer, I propose there are four key requirements for success:

1. **Intuition and Situation Awareness**, to improve agility in decision-making and execution and avoid analysis-paralysis.
2. **Smart, scientific experimentation**, to ensure tests are conducted rapidly and cost-effectively.
3. **Behavioral market research**, to define and measure fitness accurately, to drive selection and to develop intuition.
4. **An integrated approach to execution**, "Directed Opportunism", to copy and roll out selected variants rapidly and efficiently.

In Chapter 6, I examine in greater depth the requirement for speed in adaptation of the offer. This means that marketers do not want repeatedly to analyze and make explicit decisions as this slows down the process. Expert marketers develop intuitive expertise and awareness of the market situation in order to avoid slowing things down in this way. I have drawn on several recent theories of intuition in developing my recommendations for how these Test-and-Learn loops can be speeded up.

One important idea is that experts develop "Situation Awareness". This is a mental picture of the environment, against which they can check what they observe in the real environment. It allows them to foresee the results of possible actions: to model in their minds how their actions might affect the situation. This in turn allows these experts to conduct "what-if" experiments and thus build their intuition further.

However, in addition to intuition, the latest scientific tools of marketing, such as CRM, loyalty cards and prototyping also provide for rapid TLC loops in several industries. In Chapter 7, I show how a smarter approach to experimentation can be adopted using new technologies and scientific methodologies.

A further challenge in improving TLC loops is to know whether an offer is the fittest. In biology, a creature that either dies or does not reproduce has clearly not been selected. In marketing, offers need a similar way to be "winnowed out". In Chapter 8, we see how marketers can meet this challenge by adopting the right marketing metrics – metrics that are as close as possible to actual customer behavior. Recent improvements in market research, for example the expanding use of ethnography, a technique borrowed from anthropology, can help.

The final challenge, examined in Chapter 9, is to commit resources behind winning offers. If a fit offer has been identified, it is of no value if the business is unable to commit resources to rolling the offer out across the marketplace. The ability to scale new ideas and execute in an integrated way across the business is critical.

Part 4: Other Forms of Marketing

In this part of the book, I move beyond Evolutionary Marketing to examine three other forms of marketing that will, depending upon circumstance, be important. These are two non-agile approaches - Big Leap Marketing and Attritional Marketing – and one other agile approach – Maneuver Marketing.

In Chapter 10, I explore the continuing need for Big Leap Marketing. In spite of the power of agility and adaptability, Agile Marketing is not always going to suffice. Sometimes in biological evolution, the environment changes so fundamentally that existing species cannot survive through incremental change and large mutations win. Similarly in marketing, big leaps are sometimes necessary. I describe when they are worthwhile and how to ensure they are as successful as possible.

Big leaps can sometimes produce major innovations that incremental improvement will never deliver. I argue that they should however only be pursued occasionally, due to their very high risk. Specifically, innovative big leaps should be considered only when your insight into the potential innovation is so profound that the return can justify the risk. Big leaps are also necessary if the environment is changing too rapidly for your TLC loops to keep up, or if, in spite of your best efforts, market experiments are too expensive or slow, as may be the case in some industries.

Once committed to a big leap, there are two alternative approaches. The first is a more rational, measured approach to marketing that provides a rigorous way to plan the move. I describe the ADAM process, which is a four-step approach to Analyze the market situation, Decide on a plan, Act to execute against that plan, and then Measure the results. This provides a way to improve the odds of success. It also provides the base from which to move into an evolutionary phase, where fast TLC loops can help you adapt the initial plan to reflect the realities and surprises that the new environment will undoubtedly throw up.

The second approach I describe is less rational, more intuitive. It is undeniable that some well known innovations have not come from a rigorous marketing approach. Some people, such as Steve Jobs of Apple, have developed a reputation for innovation based on their own insight, not marketing analysis. I argue that whilst there are no doubt examples of this, it is far less reliable as an approach than is normally assumed. Because we concentrate on the successes, we miss the failures and we often confuse luck with skill. In short, for most readers of this book, intuitive big leaps are unlikely to further either their business's, or their own, prospects.

Executing the big leap brings a different set of challenges. I suggest that marketers can learn from the latest research on executing strategies. This brings some lessons from military history to outline how to close the inevitable gaps that arise between strategy and execution. The essence of this approach is "Directed Opportunism": in other words to ensure that those who have to execute plans are clear on the intent of the marketers, who should plan only what is necessary but no more. Those who are actually going to execute actions should do the planning, not marketers who are distant from the action. Marketers should instead set boundaries that are broad enough for the front line to take decisions for themselves and act upon them. Assuming things do not go exactly to plan, the best way to close the gap is to move from the big leap into a series of TLC loops, if at all possible.

In Chapter 11, I move away from achieving fitness either by adapting to, or shaping, the environment by improving the offer. Instead of trying to meet customer needs, a marketer can focus on beating her competition. In terms of marketing fitness, if competition has been beaten off, then the remaining player is the fittest by default.

One way to beat competition is to outspend them. I call this "Attritional Marketing." The problem with this is that it can be very wasteful, and unless you are a strong market leader, often does not work, since the market leader can spend even more. A useful analogy to understand this comes from military theory, where beating an enemy is usually the main objective. The military avoids attritional warfare unless an army has overwhelming resources.

Instead, the development of "maneuver warfare" over the past 150 years has shown the value of speed and agility in outmaneuvering an enemy. A general with an agile army can do more than adapt to the situation: he can shape the situation in his favor and surprise his enemy by acting in unanticipated ways. This in turn can demoralize the enemy and leave the general in command of the battlefield. In this way, the agile competitor can beat a more powerful one that moves slowly, so long as the mismatch in resources is not too great.

I call the analogous marketing approach "Maneuver Marketing." Using similar techniques to Agile Marketing, fast TLC loops can be applied to outmaneuver a competitor, leaving them always struggling to respond to your moves. Over time, they too can become demoralized and cede the market to you – leaving you by default with the fittest offer. This approach is little used in marketing today, although Ryanair appears to adopt this type of strategy.

As with warfare, however, this is not an approach that allows any minnow to eat the big fish – market leaders can still outspend them and often beat them that way.

Part 5: Designing the Agile Marketing Organization

I started my research trying to understand how businesses could improve their performance by becoming more customer-centric, looking at organizational change programs. In Part 5, I argue that the key to building the necessary agility into an organization is what I call a Commercial Operating System (COS), supported by a market-focused organizational structure and an appropriate company culture.

In Chapter 12, I argue that there has been a lot of work in recent years on designing structures that will help businesses be more customer-centric. I examine this work, and agree with other authors that the business needs an organization structure that fits its strategy and its competitive landscape. For large, complex businesses this should be what is known as a hybrid matrix structure. The structure should include a combination of integrators, who hold overall responsibility for the TLC loops, and specialists who can ensure true excellence in individual steps – such as experimentation or market research. There needs to be recognition of the importance of Agile Marketing, requiring greater flexibility than matrices normally achieve. Specific coordinating mechanisms need to be created to enable this.

In Chapter 13, I turn to the Commercial Operating System. All companies have a Commercial Operating System - in common vernacular the way they do marketing and sales - but very rarely do they talk about it or analyze it explicitly. This is in contrast to other functions such as production or supply chain where people will often be clear about their production operating system or their supply chain operating system.

A Commercial Operating System is a blueprint for consistent sales and marketing in the two or three functional areas (such as pricing, brand, segment, channel, or key-account management) that are most closely linked to a company's strategic priorities. It includes four main elements:

- Processes and structures
- Frameworks and tools
- Talent and Skills in Key Roles
- Metrics and Performance Management

The Commercial Operating Systems of agile organizations such as Tesco are quite different from those of traditional marketers. All four elements are aligned to improve agility. Processes and structures allow front line staff to take initiative, often based on simple, standardized processes. Frameworks and tools are developed that improve the flow of information to where it is needed, with rules of thumb to help people learn from the previous work of others. Specialist marketing skills are nurtured, while a mix of rigor and intuition is encouraged. Metrics are focused on customer behavior.

However, the continuing need for Big Leap Marketing must not be ignored, even though the Commercial Operating System to do this conflicts in some respects with agility (a system that is good at rigorous analysis of a marketplace is not the same as one that develops intuition). The trick here is to adopt an apprenticeship system of individual development. There are also benefits from combining integrators (who pull the overall marketing offer together) with specialists in particular marketing sub-disciplines, to support the necessary mix of overall situation awareness and deep expertise.

The third element of a successful Agile Marketing organization is to have an appropriate culture. In Chapter 14, I argue that it needs to encourage and inspire people to take the initiative to try new things out, to learn from the results, and to commit behind a good idea when it is shown to work. The key features of such an organization are

- An inspiring, customer focused mission
- Leading by intent, not orders
- Intuitive competence
- Mutual Trust.

Getting Started

The bulk of this book is about how, when and why to implement Agile Marketing. In the final chapter I give some thoughts on how to get started along this road. Making the change to this sort of organization is not easy, and there are few examples of companies making the shift – not least because the principles behind Agile Marketing are new. So rather than be prescriptive on how to implement a change program (something that in any case is of doubtful value), these closing thoughts consist of some observations of what has worked from various change programs in which I have been involved and how you might take these ideas forward. I propose a 6-step process, constructed as a TLC loop, to start on the journey and over time to develop your own version of Agile Marketing.

NOTES

1   Kumar, N. (2004). *Marketing as Strategy*. Boston: Harvard Business School Press.

2   Quelch, J.A and Jocz, K.E. (2008). *Greater Good: How Good Marketing Makes for Better Democracy*. Boston: Harvard Business School Press.

3   Sherrington, M. (2003). *Added value*. Hampshire: Palgrave Macmillan.

4   Kotler, P. (1991). *Marketing management* (7th ed.). Englewood Cliffs: Prentice-Hall International.

5   Clark, N. (2010, March 23) Biggest Brands: Top 100 advertisers 2010. *Marketing*

6   Brady, C.J, & Davis, I. (1993). Marketing's Mid-Life Crisis. *McKinsey Quarterly 2*, 17-28.

7   Barwise, T.P. & Meehan, S. (2004). *Simply Better.* Boston: Harvard Business School Press.

8   Kotler, P. (2004) "Marketing and the CEO: Why CEOs are fed up with marketing", *Strategy*, 3 May.

9   Nath, P. & Mahajan, V. (2008). Chief Marketing Officers: A Study of Their Presence in Firms' Top Management teams. *Journal of Marketing*, 72 (1), 65-81.

10 Lehmann, D. (2002). Quoted in "Marketers Turn to Metrics to Measure the Impact of Their Initiatives". *Knowledge@Wharton*, 14 August.

PART I

WHY HAS MARKETING FAILED TO LIVE UP TO ITS PROMISE?

The first step to answering the big question is to understand **why** marketing has failed to live up to its promise. This is obviously a complex issue, or it would have been solved in a generally accepted manner before now. I see two primary problems.

First, the promise has never been clearly defined or articulated. Marketers appear to believe that they can transform the success of businesses and many others appear to believe that they cannot, but the specifics of that transformation are rarely, if ever, articulated. The objectives of marketing have been unclear. In Chapter 2, I examine this in detail and propose a new definition of marketing and new objectives.

Second, there are tensions inherent in the promise. The environment in which marketers compete is more challenging than was anticipated by the early marketers and becoming more challenging still due to uncertainty, proliferation and demanding customers. Marketing needs to be fit, fast and efficient, but achieving all three of these is very hard. Additionally, there are tensions in how marketers should work: between intuition and rigor, between art and science. In Chapter 3, I examine these tensions and demonstrate why the new approach of Agile Marketing is required.

CHAPTER 2

A NEW DEFINITION OF MARKETING

Given the lack of clarity on marketing's objectives, I need first to define marketing clearly, including its objectives. To do this I will examine existing definitions of marketing, explore differences in understanding between marketers and strategists of what it means to compete in uncertain environments, and inspect the history of marketing over the past century.

This chapter lays the groundwork for my recommendations in the rest of the book for overcoming these challenges and managing the conflicts.

EXISTING DEFINITIONS OF MARKETING

After 25 years of practicing, researching and consulting on marketing I have come to the rather uncomfortable conclusion that we don't actually know what marketing is. Or at least, that when I describe "the promise of marketing" I am most likely talking about something quite different to what someone else might suppose. In particular, I believe that marketers mean something quite different to what other functions and CEO's mean. I suggest, however, that strategic marketing must be understood more broadly than the expectations of either of these groups.

Three dimensions

In order to arrive at a sufficiently broad definition of marketing, it is helpful to borrow from the work of strategy academics. (It is an odd fact that strategy and marketing academics are rarely well versed in each other's work, and therefore concepts in one that could be valuable to the other often gain little or no traction.) In order to understand why marketing is failing to achieve its promise, it is valuable to explore briefly the history of marketing and to understand how the general consensus amongst **marketing** academics and practitioners has begun to diverge from the perceptions of **strategy** academics and practitioners.

Three dimensions together reflect the scope of strategy: content, process and context. Content is the "what" of strategy – the course of action followed by a business in pursuit of its objectives. Process is the "how" of strategy – the way a company arrives at its strategy content. And context indicates that strategies are developed to suit varying internal situations and external environments. Three famous strategists, Porter (1980),[1] Pettigrew (1988)[2] and Mintzberg (1990)[3] each bring out this distinction, for example. It is also the structuring device used for a well-known strategy textbook (De Wit & Meyer, 1994).[4] These authors make the point that strategic management always has all three of these dimensions: they are not separate parts of strategy but rather different perspectives on strategy.

Similarly, I propose that we need to consider marketing with all three perspectives – the marketing content (what a company tries to achieve and the marketing offers it makes in the marketplace), the marketing process (how the company does this), and the marketing context (the internal context of the company doing the marketing and the environment in which it competes).

Viewing marketing strategy through these three dimensions can help us to understand the marketing promise more clearly, and therefore develop a better understanding of why it may not be achieved.

Marketers' definitions of marketing

It is an oddity that although marketing has become so widely discussed and used, there is nothing close to an agreed definition of marketing. Here are three influential definitions, one from a marketing academic and two from marketing associations. It is instructive to examine these definitions from the three dimensions of process, content and context.

The classic textbook by Philip Kotler (1994, p. 4) defines marketing in the following way:

> A social and managerial process by which individuals and groups obtain what they need and want through creating, offering and exchanging products of value to others.[5]

This definition is extremely vague. It indicates that the content of marketing is "products of value" while the goal is to ensure customers obtain what they need and want. Beyond that there is no clarity about whether this is to create profit or growth. Although calling marketing a process of creating, offering and exchanging, it is silent on some critical elements of the process: for example is marketing essentially an adaptive activity, seeking to meet pre-existing needs, or an innovative activity, seeking to create new needs? The context appears to be both "social and managerial" which is hard to decipher.

The second definition is from the American Marketing Association (AMA), the largest marketing association in North America:

> Marketing is the activity, set of institutions, and processes for creating, communicating, delivering, and exchanging offerings that have value for customers, clients, partners, and society at large.

This clearly draws on Kotler's definition, expanding it but not reducing the vagueness. The content of marketing is "offerings that have value" – which is approximately the same as Kotler's. The process dimension is broader, including "institutions" and adding "communicating" and "delivering" to Kotler's list. The context seems to cover everybody (which may in fact be what Kotler's social and managerial" meant).

Unhappy with existing definitions The Marketing Society in the UK, which bills itself as "the most influential network of over 2,700 senior marketers dedicated to championing marketing across the UK", has recently adopted the following definition as part of its *Manifesto for Marketing*:

> Marketing is the creation of customer-led demand, which is the only sustainable form of business growth.

This definition is obviously trying to relate the definition to the promise of marketing. It focuses on the content dimension (customer-led demand), without specifying what marketing does in the marketplace to create customer-led demand. It implies that the process is creative rather than adaptive, but beyond that there is no mention of process or context.

Given the vagueness and breadth of these definitions, it is perhaps unsurprising that when marketing practitioners put pen to paper, they feel the need for their own, more pragmatic definitions. For example, Mark Sherrington (2003, pp. 2-3), the former consultant and Group CMO mentioned in Chapter 1, argues that this academic form of definition fails to capture what is distinctive about marketing strategy. He believes that the difference between business strategy and marketing strategy is merely one of emphasis. He argues that from a strategic perspective, profit growth can come only from acquisitions, cost cutting or increasing revenues, and that while marketing has a role in all three, its most important role is in revenue increase – so called top-line growth. He suggests:

> Marketing is about creating top-line growth, inspiring the organization to persuade people to buy more and pay more.[6]

This focuses on the content, as does the Marketing Society. However there is an important distinction between creating growth and creating demand (demand is a property of a customer and may never be satisfied, or may be satisfied by competition; growth is a property of the organization doing the marketing). He also augments the definition by clarifying the twin goals as being to "inspire the organization" and to persuade the customer to buy more and pay more. He too, however, is silent on process, the specifics of content and the context.

Lessons from strategy

One thing the previous definitions all have in common is that they were created by experts in marketing. I thought that it might be instructive to compare and contrast these with definitions from others, for example experts in strategy. I was therefore rather surprised that "marketing" as a term hardly appears in them at all.

Whether you look at textbooks on strategy, classic tomes such as *Competitive Strategy* by Michael Porter, short "handbooks" on strategy, or more recent books seeking to identify the great new thing in strategy, they never mention "**marketing**" itself (which recall was the focus of all the marketers' definitions.) They refer instead to activities such as **market** entry and **market** signaling, measures such as **market** penetration and **market** share and objectives such as **market** dominance. The word marketing does appear in Porter's book on Page 240, six times in two paragraphs under the heading "Reduce Marketing and Selling Costs".

You might think that this omission is simply due to strategy being at a higher level than individual functions or parts of the value chain. But no! While some books did indeed have no functional references in the indices, Porter's index includes procurement, logistics and production while the handbook includes logistics and purchasing. Other books I scanned also included manufacturing.

All the books did, however, have extensive coverage of activities and concepts that marketing people think of as their own. In addition to the terms beginning with "market" mentioned above, they each mentioned segmentation, innovation, positioning and products. So strategists apparently think of marketing activities as important to strategy, but they do not link that together under the concept of marketing. On the other hand most of the marketing thinkers view marketing strategy and business strategy as broadly the same thing, except perhaps for a greater focus on top line growth, as proposed by Mark Sherrington.

Given the mismatch in perspectives between marketing and strategy writers, it is perhaps less surprising that some of the same misunderstanding appears in the world of business. Most practicing managers do not read business books. But in conversation after conversation, I find that general managers think of strategy as their domain and of marketing as a promotional activity, or sometimes as "the voice of the customer." When I describe the views of strategy embodied in the definitions from the marketing experts, I am most often met with a comment "but you are really talking about strategy, not marketing." In some industries marketing is viewed as a potential source of innovation, but almost in the same breath comes the complaint that few innovations actually emanate from the marketing function.

With this lack of shared perspective between marketers and general managers, it is hardly surprising that the promise of marketing (which we can now see is in any case only anticipated by professional marketers and marketing academics) is unfulfilled.

CEO's and other functions most often are referring to either "functional marketing" or "budgetary marketing", to use terms adopted by Tim Ambler (2000).[7] He describes functional marketing as "what marketing professionals do". This varies from company to company and may not be restricted to the marketing function, since companies sometimes disperse their marketers throughout the company. He describes "budgetary marketing", as the activities supported by a marketing budget – i.e., typically, advertising and promotion. Budgetary marketing implies a lesser scope for marketing than functional marketing.

On the other hand, marketing thinkers and practitioners are now usually talking about a still broader scope for marketing - "pan-company marketing." Ambler (2000, p. 3) describes this as "a holistic view of marketing: it is what the whole company does, not just the 'marketers', to secure customer preference and thereby achieve higher returns for the shareholder." This is a sufficiently large divergence between marketers and the rest to be worthy of further exploration.

A BRIEF HISTORY OF MARKETING

The mismatch between the views of marketers and others can be explained through a brief exploration of the history of marketing.

The first era of marketing – the selling concept

Marketing in some form has been around since the first trade was made between two humans. But in the late nineteenth century some of the features we currently associate with marketing appeared. I would characterize the first era of marketing - the period up to the mid 1950's – as "Marketing as Persuasion". During this period, marketing was primarily focused on pushing products to customers.

For example, in 1882 Procter & Gamble "conducted its first effort at mass-marketing its products through conscious consumer advertising" with a print campaign for Ivory Soaps, some 50 years after P&G first started selling soap. In 1924 it became the first company to conduct deliberate, data based market research on consumers. During the early 20th century the great mass-marketed manufacturer brands developed and became ubiquitous. Functional marketing specialists appeared in the large consumer goods manufacturers. P&G invented integrative brand management – in the "advertising department" – and other FMCG companies followed.

In 1953 the term "marketing mix" was coined by the President of the American Marketing Association, Neil Borden (a Professor at Harvard Business School), while the elements of the marketing mix were grouped together by another marketing professor, E. Jerome McCarthy, to form the well known 4P's (Product, place, price, promotion) in 1960. During this early period advertising agencies developed and flourished (the first trade association for advertisers, the American Advertising Federation, was formed in 1905). The fascination of the public with marketing was whetted by the publication of Vance Packard's "The Hidden Persuaders", 1957, a million selling popular science book.

The underlying philosophy of marketing during this era was "the selling concept". Kotler (1991, p. 16) defines this as follows:

> The selling concept holds that consumers, if left alone, will ordinarily not buy enough of the organization's products. The organization must therefore undertake an aggressive selling and promotion effort.

The selling concept is very similar to the "budgetary marketing" description of Tim Ambler. It is focused on the advertising and promotion budget. Those non-marketers who equate marketing with this are merely harking back to the early days of marketing.

The second era of marketing – target marketing

The second era of marketing began in the late 1950's, when the selling concept was usurped in the more advanced consumer companies by the "marketing concept". This business philosophy had been around before, but was only fully crystallized at this time. Kotler (1991, p. 16) defines this too:

> The marketing concept holds that the key to achieving organizational goals consists of determining the needs and wants of target markets and delivering the desired satisfaction more effectively and efficiently than competitors.

This is the philosophy of putting customers first. It was promoted by a new group of marketing academics, who explicitly contrasted marketing with selling. Peter Drucker (1973, p. 64) wrote, "The aim of marketing is to make selling superfluous."[8] His argument was that if the customer were well enough understood, he would be ready to buy, so pushing the product upon him would be unnecessary (beyond making it available). Theodore Levitt, in his classic 1960 article, "Marketing Myopia" picked up the same theme: "Selling focuses on the needs of the seller; marketing on the needs of the buyer. Selling is preoccupied with the seller's need to convert his product into cash; marketing with the idea of satisfying the needs of the customer."[9]

During this period market research developed and flourished as a discipline; unsurprisingly given the primacy of understanding the customer's needs. In the U.K., advertising agencies began to bring "account planning" - the process of combining market research with insights into the brand positioning - into their service offering, starting with Boase Massimo Pollitt in 1968. Brands and brand positioning came to the center of marketing strategy, especially following the 1980's when several major branded manufacturers were acquired for huge premiums over their book costs and at high multiples of earnings. Brand positioning became the core of marketing strategies and the concept of brand equity flourished.

In the 1970's and 1980's the scope of marketing also expanded. Trade marketing was developed in an attempt to bridge the gap that often appeared between sales and marketing functions. It sought to market to the distribution channels, thinking of them as customers with needs to be met, analogous to marketing to end customers. International marketing also developed, with the concept of "think global, act local" emerging as the primary approach.

The "marketing concept" was, by the 1990's, assumed by most practitioners and marketing academics to be the philosophy behind marketing. Building on this, "the heart of strategic marketing" was described by Kotler (1991, pp. 262-263) in the Seventh edition of his textbook as **target marketing** – namely segmenting, targeting and positioning. He commented that this was a more advanced approach to marketing than mass-marketing where all buyers get the same product but at a low cost due to economies of scale, or product-variety marketing where different features are available to provide change and variety. He also points out that while many companies were embracing target marketing, many remained wedded either to the selling concept or to the less complex forms of marketing.

The third era of marketing - holistic marketing

In the past 10 years, the concept has progressed once again. Philip Kotler and Kevin Lane Keller (his new co-author), in their most recent 13th edition of Marketing Management (2009, p. 60) introduce the "holistic marketing concept" that "recognizes that 'everything matters' in marketing – and that a broad, integrated perspective is necessary."[10] Holistic marketing combines **pan-company marketing** with **internal marketing, relationship marketing, integrated marketing**, and **performance marketing**.

In **pan-company marketing** responsibility for identifying and meeting customer needs extends far beyond the marketing department. All functions combine – across the total company system - in meeting customer needs. This concept has taken hold amongst leading marketing companies. For example:

> Diageo believes that the marketing department does not have exclusivity of wisdom. This is because everyone has an impact on consumers. Therefore they believe there is a need to give people within all departments the freedom to develop ideas and contribute to the marketing activity. The success of business depends on this. *Diageo, 2001*[11]

> Every employee of a company should consider himself or herself as part of the total company marketing effort. *Lord Marshall,* (British Airways), *Maiden Speech, House of Lords, 17th November 1998*

This trend to pan-company marketing is especially relevant in business-to-business (B2B) or industrial marketing, which has developed greatly over the past 20 years as firms have moved from the selling concept to the marketing concept. The focus of B2B marketing has increasingly been to focus on aligning the total system with customer segments. In fact, this is the natural extension of the marketing concept to a B2B business. B2B markets are not mass markets; rather the challenge is to understand small groups of customers or individuals and customize a product or service offer to them.

This move to pan-company marketing has also been prompted by the increased focus on brands and brand equity. More organizations have understood that brand leadership requires a strong alignment between the promise of the brand and the delivery of the brand. To do this, every function needs to be coordinated both in ensuring that marketing only makes promises that the organization can keep, and that the organization then actually keeps the promises.

It is striking that this move to pan-company marketing does not seem to have been understood, let alone embraced, by the whole company. How can marketers believe marketing is something the whole company does; yet everyone else thinks it is something marketers do? This conundrum leads to the next innovation: **internal marketing**. Its goal is to ensure that everyone in the organization actually embraces appropriate marketing principles (as opposed to the Board simply claiming that they do)!

There has also been in many industries a proliferation of channels that has made apparent the need to identify and manage the numerous ways in which a company may "touch" a consumer. Companies need pan-company marketing in order to integrate the customer experience across each of these touchpoints and deliver the brand promise consistently. As a consequence of this need for coordination, the third element of holistic marketing is **integrated marketing** (i.e., how to integrate the messages that a customer receives not just through traditional advertising but across media and touchpoints).

A further recent innovation is **relationship marketing**. Relationship marketing emphasizes customer retention and satisfaction. While its roots lie in the second era of target marketing, new technology in particular has dramatically accelerated its development. By understanding and responding to the needs of individual customers, the concept of relationship marketing is that businesses will be able to offer appropriate value to individuals at the right time to retain the relationship and build their loyalty. This links to the idea of pan-company marketing because the ability of the rest of the organization to respond rapidly to changes in a customer's satisfaction is critical to the concept.

A major proponent of relationship marketing, Frederic Reicheld (2001, p. 10), has written extensively on the economics of customer loyalty, arguing "an increase in customer retention rates of 5% increases profits by 25% to 95%."[12]

Relationship marketing led to CRM (customer relationship marketing) software being developed to enable more timely and informed tracking of, and communication to, individual customers. This technology has allowed new marketers such as credit card businesses and telecommunications businesses to use relationship marketing as a key business strategy. This potential has been increased many times by the rise of the Internet. By providing a new set of touchpoints, a wide range of new interactions is possible with customers. The ability to track and measure the results of these interactions once again provides the opportunity to understand and respond to customers' needs.

At the same time, relationship marketing has changed the environment in which businesses compete. Now that they know it is possible to have a 2-way dialogue with the firms that sell them things, consumers are increasingly seeking to have their say. This may be through Internet communities moderated by the company themselves, or through other forums such as Facebook. Social networking has made it clear to many companies that they can no longer control the dialogue that consumers have about their brands.[13]

Finally, **performance marketing** is really little more than demanding results from marketing, which should always have been the case. But relationship marketing, with its emphasis on measurement, has exposed what many managers believe to be a weakness in traditional marketing: that it is delivered through immeasurable and unaccountable marketing spend (the old adage that half the advertising is wasted, but nobody knows which half, is still true, but no longer viewed by many as acceptable). This in turn has led to a renewed emphasis on understanding the returns to the business from marketing activities and programs.

FIVE INSIGHTS FROM THE STRATEGISTS

Although holistic marketing is a concept that most marketing thinkers, and many marketing practitioners, would recognize and broadly accept, it is virtually unknown in the wider business world. Why do most managers ignore the holistic marketing concept? I think the answer lies in the views not only of marketing, but also of strategy. Pan-company marketing strategy as understood by marketers is very similar to what most managers think of simply as strategy. There is perhaps a greater focus on customers, but that is in practice common to many strategy discussions. And as strategy discussions increasingly embrace execution as well as planning, that leaves marketing, as Tim Ambler describes, as the execution of only either the advertising and promotion element of the marketing plan (budgetary marketing) or "what the marketing people do to implement the strategy" (functional marketing).

So the combination of the history of marketing and the evolution of strategy may explain why marketers and the rest of the organization are talking at cross-purposes when they discuss marketing and especially marketing strategy. But this does not in itself explain why the promise of marketing is not being fulfilled. Is the confusion preventing marketers from doing what they should? Possibly, but I think that the way marketers think of marketing is also insufficiently broad to fulfill the promise.

Since I am interested in strategic marketing I have looked for insights in the strategy literature that can usefully be added to the more traditional marketing literature. The aim is first to arrive at a definition of marketing that is sufficiently broad to embrace these insights and second to clarify the objective of marketing. There are five insights from strategy that I wish to highlight.

First, the insight that strategy is **competitive**. Competition really takes hold when there are scarce resources for different competitors to fight over. (If resources are not scarce, there is no need to compete – each can have whatever they want.) In marketing too, there is a scarce resource – customer spend. Of course, marketers know this, and the emphasis on market share reflects it. However there is a difference between viewing competing as a key element of what marketers actively do, as I propose, and simply viewing competition as another aspect of the marketplace to be analyzed, which is the implicit message in the definitions of marketing earlier. While competition is increasingly mentioned in real world marketing, it is striking that in Kotler and Keller less than 3% of the book (one chapter) is devoted to "dealing with competition."

Second, the **context** of strategy is extremely important. Two of the definitions mention the content perspective by giving goals for marketing – top line growth and creation of demand. None of them mentions context, since they are each supposed to apply to all contexts. However, examining marketing processes shows that context is critically important. Much of the marketing literature is preoccupied with finding best practice or identifying successful companies and initiatives and seeking to draw broader lessons from these. However, too often this work ignores the context, which leaves a fatal error. How are we to know if the "best practice" is applicable to a given context? The best management research focuses on identifying the cases in which a given lesson may be thought to apply.[14]

Third, strategists are clear about the distinction between **adapting** to the environment and **shaping** it. Michael Porter, at the very beginning of "Competitive Advantage", observes, "Competitive strategy, then, not only responds to the environment but also attempts to shape that environment in a firm's favor." He also notes that it is this ability to shape that makes the choice of competitive strategy both challenging and exciting. This distinction is not clear in the definitions of marketing, although both elements are clearly present. ("Creating demand" is a shaping content; "delivering desired satisfaction" suggests that the preference already exists.)

Fourth, one of the contextual distinctions at the heart of much strategy thinking is the degree of **uncertainty** faced by the firm. In situations where the future can be relatively accurately forecast, analytical approaches and decisive moves can be contemplated – for example in choosing whether to upgrade manufacturing capabilities for cost reductions. On the other hand where there is great uncertainty, due perhaps to technological change, scenario-based planning may be more appropriate. Marketing books, however, typically assume a high degree of predictability in their contexts. The implicit assumption seems to be that through good market research and appropriate analyses the reaction to new marketing offers can be accurately predicted. However, this flies in the face of experience and common sense. We know that most new products fail – presumably this was not the original forecast. We know that consumers continually surprise us in their reactions to advertising and direct mail. In addition, the macroeconomic environment is unpredictable – something marketers are far more sensitive to now after the credit crunch. Finally, competitors are often an additional source of uncertainty. So the degree of uncertainty in the environmental context needs to be taken account of explicitly.

Fifth, strategy thinkers and general managers have needed to spend a lot of time considering the conflicting demands of **different stakeholders**. Strategists variously argue that only shareholders matter, because they own the firm; or that shareholders, customers and employees each matter since without satisfying all of them the firm is in trouble. In addition the government is a stakeholder, both because it can tax the firm, and through regulatory intervention, which is increasing in many industries. Finally others argue that society as a whole is a stakeholder, requiring business to focus on corporate social responsibility. For example, there is now a developing point of view under the banner of sustainability that customers should not always be allowed to exercise their choices because increased consumption is bad for the environment.

This debate about stakeholders stands in stark contrast to most marketers who assert, almost as a throwaway, that business is all about satisfying customers. They have good prior support from Peter Drucker, but as we have seen this is probably too simplistic in today's complex business environment. The importance of both customers and shareholders is apparent in several of the definitions: "to secure customer preference and thereby achieve higher returns for the shareholder." Yet this craftily hides the fact that these two objectives may well be in conflict (for example, it is easy to secure customer preference by cutting price well below cost, but that does not achieve higher returns for the shareholder). You can also see the emergence of this multi-stakeholder theory in the AMA's definition: "customers, clients, partners, and society at large" but in its breadth it loses the useful specificity of "create top line growth." Kotler and Keller (2009, p. 67) also call for social responsibility in their definition of the "societal marketing concept," which enhances the marketing concept by adding in the idea of sustainability and the stakeholder of society.

> The organization's task is to determine the needs, wants and interests of target markets and to deliver the desired satisfactions more effectively and efficiently than competitors in a way that preserves or enhances the consumer's and society's long-term well-being.

So marketing theoreticians have embraced the idea of multiple stakeholders, but this idea has not really migrated into practice, nor is there much written on how to deliver the consumer imperative and still satisfy these other stakeholders.

A NEW DEFINITION OF MARKETING

In order to close the gap that has opened up between marketing and strategy, I propose a definition that embraces these five insights:

> *Marketing is the process of creating and communicating winning offers that profitably attract customer spend in an uncertain market environment. It does this by:*
> - *Shaping the market environment through innovation*
> - *Adapting to changes in the environment, and*
> - *Beating competition.*

This definition explicitly embeds the centrality of competition, sets context as a critical dimension (the market environment), focuses on uncertainty, and brings in the strategic idea of both shaping and adapting. It leaves ambiguous the role of multiple stakeholders, but as we shall see, the definition of "winning offers" can be adapted to reflect the key stakeholders.

The objectives of marketing are now clear: to shape, adapt and compete and thus to create and communicate winning offers.

In this chapter, I have exposed the gap between how marketers view the world and how strategists and many businessmen do. Marketers generally believe in a broad scope for marketing – pan-company marketing – yet this is not fully reflected in existing definitions of marketing, nor do others recognize it. This in turn has led to a mismatch of expectations and to disappointment. My new definition clarifies the expectations. The question now is: How can marketers achieve these objectives?

NOTES

1   Porter, M.E. (1980). *Competitive Strategy*. Boston: Free Press.

2   Pettigrew, A. (1988). *The Management of Strategic Change*. Oxford: Basil Blackwell.

3   Mintzberg, H. (1990). Strategy Formation: Schools of Thought. In J.W. Frederickson (Ed.), *Perspectives on Strategic Management*. New York: Harper & Row.

4   De Wit, B., & Meyer, R. (1994). *Strategy: Process, Content, Context*. St. Paul: West Publishing Company.

5   Kotler, P. (1991). *Marketing management* (7th ed.). Englewood Cliffs: Prentice-Hall.

6   Sherrington, M. (2003). *Added value*. Hampshire: Palgrave Macmillan.

7   Ambler, T. (2000). *Marketing and the bottom line*. London: Pearson Education Ltd.

8   Drucker, P. (1973). *Management: Tasks, Responsibilities, Practices*. New York: Harper & Row.

9   Levitt, T. (1960). Marketing Myopia. *Harvard Business Review*, July-August, 45-56.

10   Kotler, P. and Keller, K. L. (2009). *Marketing Management* (13th ed.) Upper Saddle River: Prentice Hall.

11   Daniels, S. (2001). *Pan-Company Marketing (PCM)*. London: The Chartered Institute of Marketing

12   Reicheld, F. F. (2001). *Loyalty Rules*, Boston: HBS Press.

13   Many marketers have argued that they never could control their brands – that in fact consumers own brands not companies. I have some sympathy with this perspective, but this previously theoretical argument is now moot. The inability to control customer dialogue is now apparent to all but the most backward marketers now.

14   For a good discussion of how this sort of research should be conducted, see Chapter 7 of Christensen, C. M., Horn, M. B., & Johnson, C. W. (2008). *Disrupting Class.* New York: McGraw-Hill.

CHAPTER 3

THE NEED FOR AGILE MARKETING

In this chapter I lay out the challenges and potential conflicts between the objectives of marketing. First, I examine how the objectives of marketing are affected by trends in the current business environment. Second, I will look at the tensions between the three goals of fitness, speed and efficiency. I believe that marketers are simply unable to use their traditional tools of segmenting, targeting and positioning to provide what customers want when the world is so uncertain and competitive. Therefore, I examine how to reconcile the apparent conflict between rigor and intuition in marketing by embracing the principles of continuous improvement and accepting a less planned approach to marketing strategy.

UNCERTAINTY, PROLIFERATION AND RAPID CHANGE

In order for marketing, as defined, to achieve its objectives it must respond to the challenges of a rapidly changing environment with proliferating complexity.

Proliferation[1] can be seen in markets, in sales and service channels, and in communications media. As customers become more demanding, segments continue to fragment. Each individual wants something more tailored to her own needs and wants. The days of the single package holiday that meets everybody's needs are over; today's traveller can put together her own flights, hotels and itinerary. Globalization adds to this trend: as we find that food from all over the world is available those of us who love Chinese expect to be catered to as well as those who love Italian. Or indeed, we now understand regional differences within countries: Szechwan food or Cantonese? Segmentation has gone far beyond the simple demographics of age and social class.

The same dynamic is apparent in B2B markets. In the past businesses would sell products to their customers who would work out themselves how to use them in their own operations. Nowadays, the rise of solutions marketing means far more tailoring of the offer to the customer's needs, while sellers require much greater understanding of their customers.

There is a similar proliferation in the number of ways businesses can sell and distribute to their customers. With greater customer demand for convenience and flexibility, most businesses now have multiple channels for sales and service. The Internet has opened up a whole new gamut of opportunities to reach customers. This in turn has led to new segmentations based on preferences for sales and distribution channels rather than preferences for product benefits. These new channels provide the opportunity to reach more customers in ways they prefer, but the experience in many industries is that cheaper channels seem to add greater cost overall to business models, as the new is added to the old rather than substituting for it. For example banks found that adding ATM's and Internet banking did not allow them to reduce the costs of their branches sufficiently, resulting in a net increase in distribution costs. Giving every customer what she wants is not affordable.

The final area of proliferation is marketing communication vehicles. The number of television channels has exploded. Most new media have arrived with business models that are based on being paid by marketers for commercials and other ways to reach potential customers. Google has rapidly become the largest media company in the world. Direct marketing has also exploded, moving beyond direct mail to email and viral marketing. Social networks and other, still to be developed, Web 2.0 applications increase the complexity yet again.

The marketing environment is also changing rapidly. Customers have become more demanding than ever before. Fifty years ago mass marketing was sufficient, because any offer was better than none; food that did not poison you was better than food that did, and advertising was a novelty often welcomed in itself. Today, customers' expectations have risen massively: there are too many offers allowing us to be more choosy, the quality of food available year round is better than ever, and we no longer tolerate poorly considered advertising that interrupts our lives. In particular, as we see an improvement in one sphere of consumption, we expect it elsewhere. For example, once McDonald's showed we did not have to wait in long queues for food, we would not tolerate long waits in other restaurants, in shops, in banks or even on the phone.

Accountability of all functions has increased as shareholders look for better returns (at the time of writing in early 2009, for any returns) from their investments. The measurability of email based direct marketing has led to renewed demands for greater measurability in all elements of the marketing mix. While the days of a Marketing Director or V.P. going to the Chief Executive and asking for $10m for a new advertising campaign "because it will improve the brand image" are probably not over entirely, there is an increasing recognition that there need to be some measurable objectives set for the campaign and that the results should be tracked.

Regulation is also on what appears to be a relentless march. Industries that have long been regulated, such as banking and insurance, are undoubtedly going to be regulated still further; food is becoming more regulated as concerns rise about obesity; retailers are threatened with being banned from opening outlets due to competition dominance at the local level and are not being allowed to reduce price on products such as alcohol on grounds of social welfare. In this context, simply focusing on consumer wants and needs is insufficient – indeed much of the problem as perceived by Government is that people are consuming too much.

Globalization is both opportunity and threat. Combined with new customer touchpoints (a term combining sales, distribution and communication channels) smaller businesses everywhere can compete properly in most countries they choose. This raises the bar for everyone, whether playing at home or away. The oft-repeated mantra of "think global/act local" also leads to its own proliferation as businesses try to manage the differences in each market without a ruinous explosion of costs.

The pace of change is also on the increase. While every genera-tion of managers seems to argue that it faces greater challenges than ever before and that the change is occurring ever more rapidly, that does not mean they are wrong. Change may come in fits and starts, but slowness in response is obviously never a desirable feature of manage-ment. Since the Boston Consulting Group published *Competing Against Time*[2] in 1990 the need for speed has increased yet further. Marketing, with its focus on adapting to the environment, is at the forefront of this.

In this uncertain, proliferating and rapidly changing world, the assumptions of traditional marketing do not hold up. It is simply unreal-istic to imagine that a mere human could see through the mists of uncer-tainty to predict not only what customers will demand in the future, but also how competitors will react. Perhaps in a simpler, gentler and more constant world market research could uncover latent demand and a small number of well-known competitors would react in predictable ways, but that is surely not the case now.

If you want to create and communicate winning offers today, you will need to take the uncertainty on board and work with it, not assume it away. You will need to revel in the proliferation. And you will need to compete to achieve your objectives.

FITNESS, SPEED AND EFFICIENCY

Marketers have always required a combination of the ability to iden-tify customer needs accurately (acuity), the ability to develop new ideas that will help them meet those needs (creativity), and the ability to deliver those ideas in the marketplace (execution). These are the inputs into the marketing process and they remain as important today as when the marketing concept was first developed.

However, in addition, if marketing is to achieve its objectives, I believe that there are two new tensions that need to be resolved. First, market-ing must respond to the complex environment with a combination of fitness, speed and efficiency. However, these three elements often come into conflict: in particular I believe that much of the work on improving marketing has tended to struggle because of the apparent trade-offs between them. Therefore any new solution needs to resolve this tension.

Second, the process of marketing is a mix of art and science; of rigor and of intuition. This mix between two apparently disparate philosophies has caught out many proponents of marketing change and caused great internal frustration to CEO's and Marketing Directors. Any new marketing process needs to acknowledge this dichotomy and accommodate it.

The increased challenges in the business environment lead to three clear requirements for marketing going forward: fitness, speed and efficiency. Fitness means meeting the demands not only of customers but also of other stakeholders, including government (either directly or through the proxy of regulation). Speed means doing so before your competition. Efficiency means doing so at the lowest possible cost.

There are many examples of companies struggling to meet these three requirements. For example, one of Tesco's competitors is Sainsbury's. After a difficult time in the 1990's and early years of the 21st century Sainsbury's new management team in 2005 found it hard to adapt to the requirements of different segments of customers. This was in contrast to Tesco, which was now using Clubcard to identify and target many such segments. Worse, Tesco was launching a continuing stream of initiatives that shaped the competitive landscape. Sainsbury's always seemed to be chasing the last initiative while Tesco was already moving on to the next. Sainsbury's could never catch up. As a result of its previous success, Tesco was also able to lower its marketing costs as a percentage of revenues due to its greater scale and the consistency of its brand message over many years, whereas Sainsbury's had gone through several different, unsuccessful advertising campaigns over the previous 15 years. Tesco had the advantage in fitness, speed and efficiency and its market share grew year after year. Only by 2008/9 was Sainsbury's able to start clawing back some of the lost ground.

An example of a company with efficiency but lacking fitness and speed was Barclaycard, the credit card operations of Barclays Bank, around the turn of the millennium. It was the largest player in the U.K.

market, having built its brand through many years of successful, high profile brand advertising. It was, however, losing share to monoline operations such as Capital One and MBNA (both new entrants from the U.S.) and retailer-based offers such as Marks & Spencer, who were able to shape the market by providing different offers to different segments. Barclaycard found itself unable to adapt to the needs of these different segments. Its marketers lacked the understanding of the market to adapt offers fast enough as the new entrants continued to shape the market. When faced with the challenge of fast, agile multi-segment competitors, Barclaycard's mass market, big brand advertising approach made it something of a dinosaur. Over the past 10 years it has had to respond by embedding a "Test-and-Learn" approach similar to that of Capital One. This proved tough, but not impossible.

Procter & Gamble, Europe found itself in a similar situation in 2000, although more due to its own actions rather than those of competitors. It reorganized by placing a European HQ in Geneva largely for reasons of tax efficiency and some regional scale. This left it with a much lower cost base than competitors. However, replacing marketers from the local markets with employees in Geneva (often much less experienced) meant a loss of focus on customers in those countries. It also meant that P&G was unable to respond as rapidly to changes in local markets, whether due to consumers, retailers or competitors. This deficit in speed led to a loss of fitness that rapidly translated into a loss of share, only reversed as a new management team refocused the organization on the consumer.

Vodafone, the mobile phone operator, faces a similar problem today in the U.K. Its competitor O2 (owned by Telefonica) has been taking share following, amongst other things, a move to SIM only packages. (In the U.K. mobile operators have traditionally funded subsidized new handsets by increasing the monthly cost of a package. But as most customers now have handsets, there is a market for just the phone calls – i.e., a SIM but no handset.) Vodafone was unable to respond sufficiently rapidly to this. Its new CEO, Vittorio Colao, said, "This is something I'm obsessed with - the speed of implementation".

The three key requirements apply equally to B2B marketers. For example, Kodak Healthcare, which sold imaging machines to hospitals, was in 2000 also challenged with fitness and efficiency. It was losing share in key segments that had been created by competition. The main problem was that its "go to market" model was not adapted to different segments. As a consequence it was under-serving some customers with its sales and service support while over-serving other segments, resulting in excess costs. In order to respond it needed to find a solution that not only adapted to these different segments, but that did so at a reasonable cost and allowed it to respond rapidly to the changing requirements imposed by governments in individual countries as well as changes in technology.

A capability that often appears in the strategy literature when considering how to combine fitness and speed is **agility**. Defined by dictionary.com as

1. The power of moving quickly and easily; nimbleness or
2. The ability to think and draw conclusions quickly; intellectual acuity,

Agility is a good summary of the approach to marketing that is demanded by the new environment.

RIGOR VERSUS INTUITION

One complication that marketing as a discipline now faces, however, is that these three requirements – fitness, speed, and efficiency – often appear to be mutually contradictory. If a marketer goes for speed, does this imply quick and dirty, forgoing efficiency of spend and quite probably fitness? If she focuses on efficiency, then there is a concern that everything will slow down while she performs the necessary analysis, while creative types may complain about being "run by accountants." In addition, many marketers argue that the key to fitness is creativity, yet managers from other disciplines believe that too often the need for creativity is used as an excuse for not learning from experience or being accountable - which would harm the ability to adapt rapidly to the environment and reduce efficiency.

As if these tensions were not enough, a marketing manager looking to develop a new approach to marketing needs to take account of a second complication. There appears to be a distinction between two quite different styles of marketing: between art and science, or between those who rely on intuition and those who rely on rigorous analysis of the facts. My own observations over the past 25 years suggest that the interactions between the three key factors for success and the two marketer styles is complex. For example, successful intuitive marketers are often able to choose very rapidly which option to take when making decisions about their offers – e.g., selecting a new product variant, choosing a new advertising spot, modifying the packaging, creating a new promotion – based largely on their own intuitive understanding both of the customer and of their own company and its products or brands. They have speed and in many respects perform well.

Conversely, analytic marketers are able to improve efficiency through a rigorous approach to measurement and analysis. But they are often criticized for analysis/paralysis leaving them susceptible to competition from more rapid competitors. For whatever reason, there seems to be more of a culture of analytic marketers in the U.S. and Germany, for example, and of intuitive marketers in the U.K.

Intuitive marketers, perhaps unsurprisingly, appear resistant to developing a rigorous, step-by-step approach to their jobs: whether it is planning a marketing strategy, developing a marketing spend program, or stimulating sales in distribution outlets. However, external reviews of their work, as we conducted at McKinsey, nearly always unearth a wide range of inefficiencies in the current spend and misallocation of resources. These intuitive marketers may have been fast and fit. But they were not efficient.

On the other hand, if they attempted to improve efficiency by adopting rigorous new processes, different problems arose. The rigor often added efficiency and fitness first time, as marketers gained greater insight into customer segments and were confronted with gross inefficiencies in their marketing activities. But over time the new processes could prove too slow and resource intensive to repeat. Consequently, in most marketing capability building programs that I observed, when marketing leaders sought to implant rigorous processes into a marketing organization, the same marketers that benefited from the one-off improvements in performance from rigor would water down the new processes over time and revert to the intuitive approach.

Considering this in light of the tensions discussed above, it is apparent that speed of action is a critical benefit of the intuitive approach, while the slowness of the rigorous approach provides the major barrier to its adoption. It is not sufficiently agile. However, on a few occasions, I saw that the marketing team adopted the new approaches and that, with practice, they could respond faster to market and competitor changes and still produce responses that went down well with customers. This shows that the rigorous approach, once fully internalized, is not necessarily slower or less agile. The difference lies in the organization and the culture, as we shall see in Part 5.

CONTINUOUS IMPROVEMENT AND EMERGENT STRATEGY

Reflecting on these observations, the challenge for a new approach to marketing is to combine the speed of intuitive marketers with the efficiency of analytical marketers, while always seeking to be fit in the competitive environment. There are two further insights from strategists that can help in the search for a new approach.

The first is the strategic importance of continuous improvement. The experience curve, first discussed by the Boston Consulting Group in the 1960's, embeds the idea of continuous decline in costs in an industry. Due to experience and learning, costs fall in a predictable manner. This continuous improvement results in price declines over time, while competitors whose costs do not fall in this way rapidly become uncompetitive and fail or leave the industry. Over the past 30 years continuous improvement has become core to the operating functions of manufacturing and logistics. Tools such as Lean Manufacturing and Six Sigma have enabled businesses to continue this improvement in costs.

The parallel concept of continuous improvement in marketing is embedded in the price/value curve. This demonstrates that at any point of time the price a customer would be willing to pay for an offer is related to the value she perceives in the offer. Over time, the value tends to increase as businesses compete to improve the offer, while the price tends to fall through the experience curve. However there is no marketing process to parallel Lean Manufacturing that will ensure continuous improvement.

The second learning from the strategy field is that in management there may not be a "right answer" for how to do marketing. In strategy there is no dominant mainstream as there is in some other fields. Strategic management is fragmented into competing schools of thought. One particular dichotomy is between "deliberate strategy" and "emergent strategy." The former focuses on planning, direction and control – getting desired things done – the latter opens up the notion of learning what works by taking one step at a time. In reality, no strategy approach is likely to be purely deliberate or emergent, but rather to lie on a spectrum between them. Marketing thinking on the other hand is dominated by deliberate marketing – planning what needs to be offered and getting people to do it.

I do not doubt that deliberate marketing strategy has its place in business. Indeed, much of Part 4 of this book is focused on it. However, an agile approach to marketing – one that combines the principles of continuous improvement and emergent strategy – will help marketers achieve their goals far more often. The focus on learning from experience and adapting all the time answers the challenges I have posed in this chapter.

In short, I believe that the lack of an emergent, continuous improvement approach to marketing is the main gap in marketing theory. That gap is what my theory of Agile Marketing seeks to close.

In Part 1, I have explored the history of marketing and lessons from the theory of strategy to arrive at a new definition of marketing.

Marketing is the process of creating and communicating winning offers that profitably attract customer spend in an uncertain market environment. It does this by:
- *Shaping the market environment through innovation*
- *Adapting to changes in the environment, and*
- *Beating competition.*

This in turn clarifies the objectives of marketing as the development of fit offers in an uncertain, competitive environment, achieved through a combination of shaping, adapting and competing. In a marketing environment that is becoming increasingly uncertain with greater proliferation and rate of change, the bar has been raised for fitness, speed and efficiency. A new, agile approach to marketing is required, an approach that combines intuition and rigor where appropriate. This approach must be emergent rather than deliberate and continuously improving rather than a big leap. The next Part outlines how the theory of evolution can meet these multiple needs.

NOTES

1   Webb, A. P. (Ed.). (2006). *Profiting from Proliferation.* New York: McKinsey & Company.

2   Stalk, G. Jr. & Hout, T. M. (1990). *Competing Against Time.* New York: Free Press.

PART 2

INTRODUCTION TO EVOLUTIONARY MARKETING AND TEST, LEARN, COMMIT LOOPS

In the mid-19th Century, the search for an explanation of how biological species could develop and adapt through continuous improvement led Charles Darwin to the theory of evolution by natural selection. In Part 2, I explain how the 21st century search for an explanation of how marketing offers could develop and adapt through continuous improvement can also be resolved through a theory of natural selection. The essence of this approach is to implement a continual loop of **test**ing marketing offers, **learn**ing which are the best and then **committ**ing to those winners before repeating the loop. This approach – that I call Evolutionary Marketing, is the most common form of Agile Marketing.

In Chapter 4, I expound the theory of Evolutionary Marketing and Test, Learn, Commit loops. In Chapter 5 I illustrate the practice of Evolutionary Marketing through two case studies, Tesco the UK-based grocer and Capital One, the credit card company.

CHAPTER 4

EVOLUTIONARY MARKETING – TEST, LEARN, COMMIT LOOPS

In this chapter I examine the theory of evolution and how it can be applied to marketing.

THE ESSENCE OF EVOLUTION

Evolution began life (as it were) in biology, but has since expanded into other domains.

Evolution in biology

We have become familiar with evolution as a theory of change in biology. As I write this it is both the 200th anniversary of Darwin's birth and the 150th anniversary of the publication of his great work, *On the Origin of Species by Means of Natural Selection, or the Preservation of Favoured Races in the Struggle for Life.*[1]

In this book Darwin (1859) noted that resources were limited for populations and that therefore a struggle for survival was bound to ensue. The survivors would be the fittest: those best adapted to the environment at that time. He extended earlier ideas of transmutation of species (i.e., that creatures change over time) by developing an outline of HOW that change could occur. At its simplest, this is through three linked processes: variation, selection and replication (or reproduction).

Darwin argued that the key to success in an evolutionary system is to be good at creating **variation** within a population, **selection** of the fittest variants, and **replication** of the selected variants to ensure they increase their share of the population.

The idea was that from an individual, a number of different variants were created. These variants then each tried to survive in the environment. Those best adapted to the environment survived; the less fit were winnowed out. Finally, it was necessary to replicate the fit characteristics, so the survivors needed to reproduce. This ensured that there were more of the fit variants remaining in the population for the next generation to go round the loop. In this way the population would be able to capture a greater share of the total resources available in the environment. But because the environment, and competition, is always changing this process of evolution must be continual.

It is worth noting that Darwin did not know the mechanism by which variation could be created and inherited by individual creatures. The combination of the theory of natural selection with the theory of Mendelian inheritance, which brought the concept of genes as the mechanism, did not occur until the 1930's. He simply concluded that there must be such a mechanism. This suggests that the theory of natural selection does not depend on genetics to be applicable.

Darwin's work has, we all know, become the foundation of modern biology and been incomparably influential in that sphere. However it is less well known that since Darwin's day, we have come to realize that the essence of Darwin's ideas can apply to fields of study beyond biology. In particular, the theory of evolution through natural selection has been applied in the field of economics, while the mathematics behind the theory has been developed in ways that greatly increases its scope.

In order to apply the theory of natural selection in non-biological domains, we need to draw out the core elements of the theory. In addition to the three core processes of variation, selection and replication, there are three underlying elements. First, the theory is based on the existence of "interactors": entities that interact with each other and with the environment. They do the living and dying over time (organisms in biology). Second, the theory requires that there are scarce resources and competition for those resources amongst interactors. Third, the fitness of an interactor, that determines how successful it will be in competition for scarce resources and whether it is suited to survival in that environment, is hard to predict and indeed is determined not only by the environment but also by other interactors that exist at that time.

Evolution in economics

Evolutionary economics is a small but growing discipline within economics that explicitly focuses on the dynamics of market places and organizations. This has been developed in response to two major difficulties in classical economics.

First, classical economics assumes that systems are in, or moving towards, equilibrium. This is because the mathematics behind classical economics looks at steady state maxima and minima, identifies when variables are in balance (for example supply equaling demand) and basically assumes that if things are changing it is because things have got out of balance. However this does not match with experience in business, which is a world of almost constant change – if anything is ever in balance any businessman will assume that it will shortly be out of balance again.

The second major difficulty in classical economics is the assumption of perfect rationality. In order for the theories of microeconomics to work, the concept of *Homo economicus* has been developed. This paragon of rationality is able to integrate all the information about a situation that is available to him, calculate the necessary probabilities and utilities of all possible actions he might take, rationally choose the best decision and then subsequently act upon that decision. This too does not match the real world, where people get confused, make mistakes, act on their emotions, take short cuts in their reasoning and generally act like *Homo sapiens* rather than *Homo economicus*.

Evolutionary economics dispenses with these assumptions, instead viewing economic activity as one where businesses and institutions evolve in ways analogous to how creatures evolve in biology. In fact, the mathematics of classical economics can be replaced by the mathematics of evolution, if the same core elements are present – which they are.

First, the interactors in economics are business units – they live and die and compete in the market place. Second, these business units are competing for scarce resources in terms of capital for funding, revenues from customers, and employees from talent pools. Third, fitness is defined by success in these three marketplaces, while the competitive environment is hard to predict and ever changing, such that a winning strategy is far from obvious. The three core processes of evolution also apply: there is variation created both through innovation as well as random chance in a business; differences in performance between businesses result in organizational growth or decline – i.e., selection; and successful business ideas are replicated both in the originating organization and in other businesses through the transfer of "best practice", thus ensuring replication.

Since the same elements are in place, the mathematics of this economics is the same as the mathematics of biological evolution, and much of the intuitive reasonableness of the theory comes in analogy to biological evolution. This mathematics relates closely to some theories of complex adaptive systems, which is where the ideas of "chaos theory" emanate from. The idea of "creative destruction," much discussed during the credit crunch, holds that capitalism destroys businesses that are no longer fit for the current environment, replacing them with new, fitter ones. This is "survival of the fittest" – an idea straight from evolution.

Of course, while the mathematics of evolution can be applied to this different domain, that does not mean that everything in biology directly translates. In fact, it is dangerous to push the analogy with biology too far: e.g., firms do not have sex! It may be fun intellectually to look for the analogy to sex – e.g., M&A, or customer/suppler relationships, and then to discuss what businesses might do (e.g., make themselves look more attractive to partners) but that is NOT the point of evolutionary economics. Rather we observe that businesses do replicate their successful processes, which is all that is needed to apply the lessons of evolution. This is more than an analogy – the claim is that businesses really do evolve through natural selection. "The Origins of Wealth" by Eric Beinhocker (2006)[2] is an excellent (long) introduction to this field, which has been particularly strong in understanding changes in management practices over time, the relationship of these changes to new technologies and how these can lead to economic growth.

Evolution in marketing

To my knowledge, nobody has yet extended this thinking directly to marketing, although the idea of marketing evolving is beginning to emerge in the literature in an informal way.

A natural by-product of evolution of businesses is evolution of parts of businesses, i.e., of functions. In order to show that natural selection can apply to marketing, just as to the broader field of economics, I need to demonstrate that the activities of marketing contain the elements that allow us to apply these evolutionary ideas. They are embedded in my definition of marketing presented in Chapter 1:

> *Marketing is the process of creating and communicating winning offers that profitably attract customer spend in an uncertain market environment. It does this by:*
> - *Shaping the market environment through innovation*
> - *Adapting to changes in the environment, and*
> - *Beating competition.*

In this definition,
- The interactor is a commercial offer (product and/or service) that competes for selection amongst customers.
- These commercial offers are competing for the scarce resource of customer spend in the marketplace.
- Fitness is defined not only by how attractive the value proposition of the marketing offer is to potential customers in the market - but also by the attractiveness of the overall offer to the other stakeholders, e.g., by creating profit for shareholders, fitting the aspirations of employees or the social responsibility requirements of local communities.
- This occurs in an uncertain environment that is hard to predict as customers and competitors change their minds and react to each other, often very rapidly.
- Variation is achieved by modifying marketing offers - together with random chance causing a myriad of minor changes.

- Selection is defined by the attractiveness of the overall value proposition to customers and to the other stakeholders, in particular by creating profit.
- Replication is through individual learning, company wide adoption of successful practices, and copying from other companies' successes - both directly, through ad agencies and consultants, and through transfer of employees.

Since the core elements of evolution apply to marketing, we can adopt the entire theory. In other words, the three core processes of variation, selection and replication can be applied to a marketing offer and over time the offer will evolve in the same way that biological creatures do.

Importantly, this also means that many lessons learned from biological and economic evolution can be applied to marketing. For example, in biology very large changes to creatures can happen over time, far greater than one might have imagined, given the incremental nature of each change. Similarly, applying the evolutionary approach to a business's marketing offers should allow it to adapt those offers to the marketplace, however uncertain the consumer demand or competitive activity. To understand why this is so, it is helpful to introduce one additional new concept – the fitness landscape.

THE FITNESS LANDSCAPE

Evolution through natural selection can be thought of as a "search for fitness". In other words, in an ecosystem, every possible creature has a certain level of fitness. Natural selection is a way to search among these possible creatures to find ones with higher fitness. Pictorially, Figure 4-1 represents this.

A fitness landscape

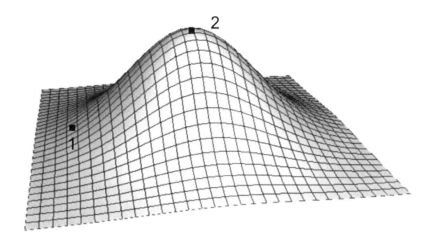

Figure 4-1

This landscape describes how fit different creatures are – at any given point of the landscape, the height of the surface above the base is the fitness. Then where we would most like to be on this landscape is at Point 2. If fitness were purely defined by share of customer spend, Point 2 would be where there is the greatest potential to capture share of customer spend (although as I argued earlier, in reality fitness is more complex, encompassing the demands of multiple stakeholders).

Suppose we start at Point 1 – the question is how do we find point 2? Although it is drawn like a mountain landscape, note that unlike real world mountain landscapes, this fitness landscape is continually shifting and changing. In particular, other interactors that actually exist can affect it. For example, if a new very fit interactor is created that captures all the scarce resources, previously fit interactors will immediately become unfit. Therefore an interactor not only adapts to the fitness landscape but also shapes it. One executive I discussed this with suggested the landscape should be thought of more like waves in a sea, continuously changing in apparently unpredictable ways.

Problems with searching the fitness landscape the traditional way

In traditional, needs-based marketing, we might conduct market research to understand consumers' needs and wants, perform some competitive analysis to assess the likelihood that they could execute certain offers, create a plan to move our offer to the place we have identified as Point 2, and then execute against that plan. The problem with this approach, in the rapidly moving world of many consumer industries, such as grocery retailing, is that it is very unlikely to work.

Why not? First, our market research is subject to all sorts of potential inaccuracies, due not to incompetence of the researchers but rather human uncertainty amongst consumers. *Homo sapiens* (as opposed to *Homo economicus*) is not reliable at predicting how he will react when a real-life marketing offer is made to him. Innovators throughout the ages have noted this. Akio Morita is famous for saying that market research would never have come up with the Sony Walkman:

> *"Carefully watch how people live, get an intuitive sense as to what they might want and then go with it. Don't do market research."*

More recently Steve Jobs has been quoted as arguing that Apple needs to lead the consumer rather than follow them:

> *"You can't just ask customers what they want and then try to give that to them. By the time you get it built, they'll want something new."*

Market researchers have come up with ever more realistic ways to probe the true needs and wants of consumers – most recently the growth of ethnographic research is an example of this trend. But if consumers do not know how they will react, it will be impossible to elicit the information.

Second, even if we knew exactly how consumers would react, we could not predict the actions of competitors. Here too, this is not due to incompetence but rather an inherent unknowability. There are theories in classical economics based on rational choice, game theory and complicated differential equations, but these always entail massive simplification of the competitive environment. Furthermore, real life competitors often do odd things (being run by members of the species *Homo sapiens, not Homo economicus*).

Third, even if we did know exactly what customers and competitors would do, our own actions are far from certain. Actually delivering exactly what our plans require is basically impossible in large organizations. Again, this is not due necessarily to incompetence (although it might be!) but rather the limitations of the capabilities of real life companies and the difficulty of information flow of exactly what is required from the center to the front line. In fact, very often the planned offers may never have been deliverable in the first place. For example, the provider of simulated test markets, BASES, combines consumer reaction to new product initiatives with marketing plan information to forecast likely sales volume. However in conversation with their consultants, they reveal that one of the major sources of error in these forecasts is that the innovating company does not execute the marketing plan as provided. Advertising spend levels may be less, distribution of the product may vary, and pricing levels may change. Each of these affects fitness.

Just in case this is not enough to convince you that the traditional needs-based approach faces problems, there is a myriad of additional uncertainties. The government may change regulations, there may be a major change in the economic environment, or a new health scare might increase risk aversion amongst customers. There is simply too much uncertainty for management to be confident in this approach.

Searching the fitness landscape with natural selection

Fortunately, natural selection provides an alternative way of climbing to the peak of the fitness landscape. It is a search approach, consisting of a sequence of actions that can be followed repeatedly, that moves upwards step by step. If a company wishes to apply natural selection, it must have an initial offer, which is the starting point. It first adjusts some of its marketing tactics, thereby creating several variations on its initial offer, which can be shown pictorially as different lines on the fitness landscape (Figure 4-2). Then it selects the new variation that is most fit and rejects variations if they are less fit. Pictorially, that corresponds either to moves upwards or to staying at the same level. Of course after just one step, we have not moved far towards Point 2.

The first cycle of natural selection

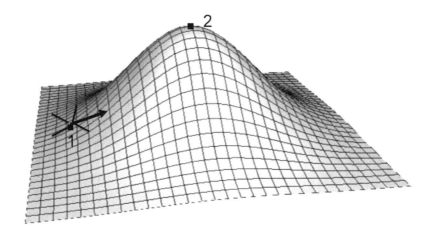

Figure 4-2

The company then repeats the process from the new starting point. At each step it explores in the vicinity of the starting point, and over time it is certain to move upwards unless it is already at the top, in which case it will stay there. So with this sequence of variation followed by selection, evolution develops ever more "fit" marketing offers driven by ever more appropriate marketing tactics (Figure 4-3).

Natural selection

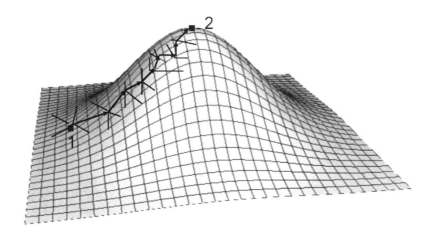

Figure 4-3

The big attractiveness of this approach is that you do not need to know where you are going – you simply move upwards until you can go no further. This property is critical to biological evolutionary theories, where one aim of the theory is to explain how very complex organisms can evolve that are fit in their environment without some entity giving directions to the top. My contention is that in the rapid moving, complex environments of consumer marketing, no one truly knows where they are going, and that the evolutionary algorithm is equally an efficient way of finding the peaks. Here, after eight steps the offer has reached the peak at Point 2.

This is the essence of Evolutionary Marketing. It is the most common form of Agile Marketing, although as we shall see in Chapter 6 there are some forms of Agile Marketing that do not follow the evolutionary model.

Evolutionary Marketing may seem to be a long, slow process compared to the "point and shoot" approach of classic target marketing – which I call "Big Leap Marketing." After all, as in Figure 4-4, the other company reached the peak faster, perhaps giving it first-mover advantage.

Continuous improvement vs. Single shot innovation

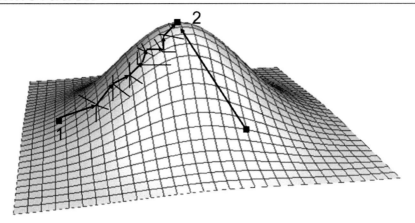

Figure 4-4

Continuous Improvement:		Single Shot:
• Search for the peak (2) by improving a small amount every step • Guaranteed never to get worse	VS.	• Try to identify optimum "from afar" • Plan how to reach it • Commit resources to execute plan

However this does not take account of the uncertainty and complexity in the environment. If there were no uncertainty and you were able to analyze the landscape completely, then indeed it would be better simply to jump to the peak. But where there is uncertainty, due either to the landscape itself or your inability to analyze it completely, the range of error becomes more important.

Evolutionary Marketing vs. Big Leap Marketing

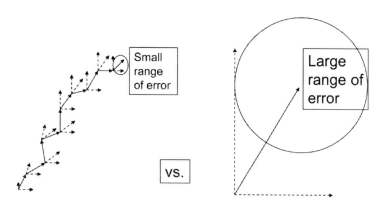

Figure 4-5

As Figure 4-5 illustrates, taking a series of small steps and selecting the fittest each time dramatically reduces the range of error from the single shot approach of Big Leap Marketing. It is like an aircraft pilot continuously correcting the course en route to the peak as opposed to simply programming the autopilot to fly where he believes the peak to be, ignoring any chance of being wrong, of setting the course or velocity slightly wrong, or being blown off course. The greater the uncertainty, the more benefit from the evolutionary approach.

One word of warning is appropriate here, however. The previous diagrams suggest that a sequence of small moves will always succeed. But this is not true, due to the problem of "local optima". An example of this can be seen if the fitness landscape is a bit more complex, as in Figure 4-6. If you start at Point B this local peak has no small moves that are up. If you want to move from Point B, it may not be possible to do it step by step, because each move is initially down, and thus will tend to be selected against. However it is more risky to take larger steps as these could move into valleys that are so deep as to result in elimination of the offer (death in biology, failure of a product offer). So occasional higher risk leaps followed by new smaller steps could be a way to find peak 1 from Point B, perhaps via Point A.

When evolution does not work

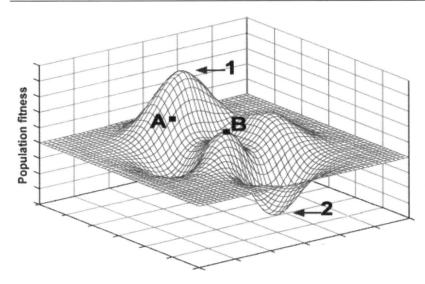

Figure 4-6

In biology we know that occasional large mutations are an important part of the overall evolutionary process. We will return to this need to balance between large and small steps in marketing in Chapter 5.

Finally, even where there is no risk of local optima, it may be desirable to combine the two methods of Evolutionary Marketing and Big Leap Marketing. If you believe you have a relatively good idea of what the best offer might be, you could search the landscape by an initial big leap followed by a series of evolutionary steps to reduce the margin of error. In fact, I believe that if you have made such a big leap you should **always** try to follow it by Evolutionary Marketing if possible, since it is much more likely that you will land on the "foothills" of the peak you are searching for (such as Point A in Figure 4-6).

TEST, LEARN, COMMIT LOOPS

In order to apply natural selection to marketing offers, businesses need to be able to execute the three core processes of variation, selection and replication. The essence of the first two of these is already present in many businesses in the form of test-and-learn processes. The additional need for replication is met through a process of committing resources to the selected variants. The combination of these processes into Test, Learn, Commit loops is the main approach I propose to adapt to the marketplace. These loops are at the core of Evolutionary Marketing.

Just as with biological evolution, marketers start from an existing offer and create variations by **testing** new offers. They then measure what works by identifying metrics for each variant. From what they **learn**, one or more of these variations are selected for further **tests** to create another set of variants and the marketers **learn** some more. Again some of the variants are selected. Once the business is satisfied with the fitness of the selected variant, it winnows out the failures and copies the winners by **committing** significant resources to rolling out the successful offers into the marketplace. Immediately the business also embarks on testing new variants of the committed variant in order to improve fitness still further. The process then repeats over and over.

How to conduct Agile Marketing: Test, Learn, Commit (TLC) loops

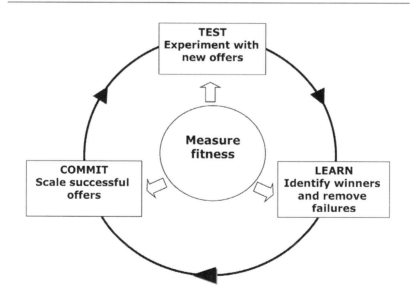

Figure 4-7

Let us first examine each of the elements of these Test, Learn, Commit loops, before giving two case examples of businesses that already work this way

Test

Marketers have traditionally been able to create a huge array of variations. In new product development (NPD) there have been numerous line extensions and high profile launches. Advertising is notorious for frequent changes and a cult of creativity. Promotions create variety in pricing; salesmen are always looking for a new gimmick; there is an ongoing search for new distribution outlets.

However, simply creating variations is only the starting point for evolution. Indeed, evolution in biology is an inherently wasteful process. Darwin's genius was to demonstrate how random variation could lead to brilliantly adapted creatures. The biologist Richard Dawkins (1986) contrasted the differences between human design and its potential for planning with the workings of natural selection.[3] A Creationist argument by a Reverend Paley (1802) had earlier used the analogy of a watchmaker (the argument was that just as the existence of a watch compels belief in a watchmaker, so existence of mankind compels belief in a divine creator).[4] Dawkins argued that evolutionary processes were analogous to a blind watchmaker, because in fact the theory of evolution by natural selection shows that extremely complex designs can be generated by evolution. But, being blind, the process absorbs enormous resources and takes a very long time.

Marketers have a major advantage since they are not, usually blind, but rather can engage in "thoughtful tinkering."[5] In other words they can use their insights into the marketplace to make judgments about where the fitness landscape goes "up" as a guide to which variants to create. But if they rely too much on these judgments, then they risk undermining the evolutionary algorithm (because if their judgment is flawed, all the variants may be less fit and they will never explore in the right directions). So the trick is to combine their insights with some random experimentation. As we shall see, marketers using Test, Learn, Commit loops are often surprised by what actually works better, demonstrating the value of some tinkering without much thought.

I will examine in the next chapter how companies can improve their judgments for creating variations, as well as give ideas for reducing the cost and time taken to experiment. For now, it is important to note that variations need to be able to be selected through a measure of fitness. It is not enough simply to change things; the variants must be subject to as close a version of the true marketplace as possible. The challenge with "Test" is to find ways of experimenting cheaply and rapidly, while remaining as true as possible to the market environment.

Even with this constraint, the potential for improvement in testing is vast. Already, companies are using panels of creative consumers to help in the ideation phase of new product development (NPD). Companies, especially in the technology area, involve agencies to facilitate what they call "co-creation" sessions with these creative consumers, their own NPD/design teams and external NPD agencies. However, testing at its best is more than simply developing ideas; businesses need to develop prototypes to simulate actual usage as closely as possible. Here too massive strides are being taken. For example, Nokia is able to think up and try out new phones with real consumers on a fast turnaround at low cost. Similarly, new technology has meant that testing through simulation can be far more meaningful than ever before.

Learn

In order to meet the overall marketing criteria of fitness, speed and efficiency, it is not desirable to copy every variation across the entire market. Learn is the stage in the loop where this is avoided. It depends critically on measurement and on reviewing results against clear objectives. I believe that this is the weakest element of the Test, Learn, Commit loop for many marketers.

For example, over 90% of new products in fast moving consumer goods fail. I would argue that this is the result of poor learning. Since many of these new products (variations) have had to incur high fixed costs throughout the supply chain as well as frequently in marketing communications, this commitment to unfit variants is incredibly wasteful.

In some industries learning can be achieved through realistic trials. For example, in retailing, a new merchandise offer or a price experiment can be conducted in store with little or no impact on the broader chain. The Test-and-Learn parts of the loop can be repeated as many times as required, the business can copy only the successful ones, and the experiments can be continued through further Test-and-Learn trials.

In other industries it may seem impossible to learn through marketplace trials – for example project-based B2B marketing, or in industries such as electricity retailing. But with creativity it is usually possible to get closer to a valid learning approach than currently. For project based B2B it is possible to "float" possible offers in the dialogue with a client to gauge attractiveness, as well as to try out bolder ideas on clients where you are not too bothered about getting the business. In electricity retailing, there may be a concern that competitors will copy your moves, but using CRM techniques offers can be made to a small number of consumers in ways that are impossible for the competition to observe or track.

The reality of many marketing departments is that their tests are not subject to rigorous learning. The reason why this is especially important is that it brings to the fore a second main process in evolution. In addition to "natural selection" there is also "drift". This reflects how populations evolve when due to randomness there are variants that are less fit but nevertheless survive. (At its simplest, assume that you are far more fit a creature than I am. Through natural selection, you ought to reproduce better than me – but if you are run over by a bus before you do so, I win. Game Over!)

Evolutionary economists have shown that when there is not a "sharp" fitness function (i.e., when selection is often left to chance rather than a clear definition of fitness) then drift can lead to evolution decreasing fitness over time – even eliminating desirable processes and business models entirely. Similarly, in order for evolution to increase fitness, marketers must put in place sharp selection through rigorous and objective learning. This has often not been the case, not least because it can be very hard.

The most obvious example is in broadcast advertising, when most marketers believe that effectiveness cannot be measured. Consequently there is lots of variation but no real tests, while learning is limited, due either to a total lack of measurement or measurement of criteria only slightly related to true fitness. Logically this will mean that drift dominates over natural selection and broadcast advertising will not be a well-adapted part of the marketing offer in many situations. In other words, broadcast advertising will not evolve successfully. As we shall see in the next chapter that means in particular that it will likely not be as efficient and effective as other, more measurable marketing tools and will lose share of marketing spend to them.

We will see later that the key to speed and efficiency in learning is to retain outstanding awareness of the market situation and of which offers are fit and not fit. This in turn requires clear objectives and metrics, immersion in the environment to improve judgment and the development of rules of thumb to select offers in a given marketplace.

Commit

Commitment is where the decision is taken to invest the business's resources in a new offer.[6] This is in some ways separated from the Test-and-Learn parts of the loop because it is often more "strategic" and people at a higher level of the organization will usually execute it. It will often involve far broader implementation and delivery challenges than the initial "Test-and-Learn" process.

In traditional terms, this may not be seen as a marketing process at all, if we are referring to the overall product or service offered by the company.[7] However with my definition of marketing, delivery of the offer is key, not just having the idea. The key to speed and efficiency in committing resources is to have outstanding executional capabilities, both to kill unsuccessful experiments fast and to roll out selected variants through the business system.

This is where Evolutionary Marketing differs from most current versions of Test-and-Learn marketing. Many proponents of Test-and-Learn can identify offers that would work in the marketplace, only to discover that they cannot execute them. This is often found, for example, in service organizations such as banks. It is one thing to identify how a bank clerk should greet a customer and enquire about whether there are additional services that the customer might value from the bank. It is quite another thing for every one of the 50,000 clerks to do this as envisaged by the marketer. An example of this process going wrong was when I went into a branch to cash a check and was politely asked whether I wanted a 25-year mortgage, something that could not have been further from my mind.

Three critical requirements for successful commitment are good **communication** between the marketers and the decision makers, **integration** of operations between marketing and other functions and the **ability to scale** up delivery operations rapidly.

- The importance of good communications between the Test-and-Learn" stages of the loop and the Commit step is to ensure that the proposal to commit resources is seen in context of the lessons learnt from the first two steps. If this is missing, then innovative ideas may be lost due not to lack of fitness but to lack of understanding. For example, the store manager of a clothing retailer experimented with various ways of displaying children's clothes and saw a significant uplift in sales with one particular merchandising plan. She tried to explain what she had done and why she thought it worked to Head Office. However this company had poor communication between the stores and the main buyers and marketers, largely because it believed that the job of store managers was simply to execute what they were told. Unsurprisingly, far from being rewarded for her initiative and the new ideas rolled out across the chain, she was reprimanded for deviating from the agreed plan.

- The importance of integration between marketing and other functions is best illustrated in B2B marketing. For example, a large market research agency identified through some pilots a new offer combining some revised IT and a more knowledgeable customer service approach, at a premium price, that would be particularly attractive to its core clients. The plan was to roll this out across all its core clients and countries. Unfortunately, both the customer service staff and the technical developers struggled to implement the new offer, even though the marketers were able to articulate the promise clearly. Consequently the clients were more dissatisfied after the announcement of the new offer (which in reality was never properly launched). It was no surprise when the agency was taken over the following year.

- Finally, Google illustrates the importance of scalability. Google has a relentless focus in its marketing efforts on viewing things from a user's perspective (as opposed to its advertisers). Its philosophy is to launch early, aggressively review all the facts, refine, but always be 'in beta' with any product (i.e., the Test, Learn, Commit loop continues). Google puts new offers out into the marketplace and then uses the facts to refine its early efforts, in order to meet clear objectives. But none of this would create a great business if it did not have the capacity to scale the successful variations.

  As reported by Iyer & Davenport (2008, p. 60),[8] Google has:

> "… made major investments to get more out of it [the Internet] and to construct a proprietary platform that supports new and growing online services. According to unofficial but widely reported statistics, Google owns a network infrastructure consisting of approximately one million computers; these run an operating system that allows new computer clusters

to plug in and be globally recognized and instantly available for use."

Furthermore, the platform is built to scale further, so that as more data storage, analytical capacity or bandwidth is required, it can be easily added. This article was published in April 2008; you can be sure that this capacity has increased significantly since then. As a consequence of this scale and the platform flexibility that makes it relatively easy to roll out new ideas, Google is able rapidly to dominate new markets it enters. By being able to commit to its best ideas, it gets the maximum value out of its Test-and-Learn approach.

In this chapter I have shown how evolution can be described as a series of Test, Learn, Commit cycles. While its best-known application is to biology, it has also been applied to economics and now to marketing. We have seen how it can be viewed as an approach to continuous improvement in marketing. By thinking of marketing as a search in the fitness landscape for peaks, Evolutionary Marketing can reduce the margin of error for marketers as they try to improve their offers. Evolutionary Marketing is the most common form of Agile Marketing, standing in stark contrast the more common Big Leap Marketing. Nevertheless, Big Leaps may sometimes be an important part of the marketing toolkit.

Turning to how businesses can implement Agile Marketing, I went through each of the steps of Test, Learn and Commit. Testing depends on creating experimental variants. There should be enough variants to allow a proper search of the fitness landscape and they should be conducted rapidly and cheaply. Learning depends on having a good fitness measure, which typically means behavioral information as close as possible to real life. Commitment is the key to ensuring that selected variants become the new generation of offer. It requires good communication between marketers and decision makers, integration of operations between marketing and other functions and the ability to scale up operations rapidly.

NOTES

1   Darwin, C. (1859). *On the Origin of Species.* London: John Murray.

2   Beinhocker, E. D. (2006). *The Origin of Wealth.* Boston: HBS Press.

3   Dawkins, R. (1986). *The Blind Watchmaker.* London: Longmans.

4   Paley, W. (1802). *Natural Theology.* Reissued (2009). Cambridge: Cambridge University Press.

5   Beinhocker (2006) refers to deductive tinkering.

6   This is true in the first mode of TLC (Agile Marketing). There is a different mode, Maneuver Marketing where the situation differs, as will be seen later.

7   If we are referring to part of the marketing mix, the decision may remain within marketing, but still be referred up to the next level, e.g., from advertising manager to brand manager.

8   Iyer, B. & Davenport, T.H. (2008). Reverse Engineering Google's Innovation Machine. *Harvard Business Review* (April), 58-68.

CHAPTER 5

TWO CASE STUDIES

CAPITAL ONE

An example of a company able to execute Test, Learn, Commit loops is Capital One, the credit card company, that is now the 4th largest issuer of Visa and Master-cards in the US. Its marketing approach is based on an Information Based Strategy (IBS) which allows it to "mass customize the company's products by building massive databases of consumer information and by transforming our company into a scientific testing laboratory…we can deliver the right product to the right customer at the right time and at the right price".[1]

Before Capital One started up in 1989, the U.S. credit card industry was highly profitable and relatively uncompetitive, even though the majority of people already had credit cards and more than 4,000 banks issued them. Banks charged the same APR for all customers and the same annual fee.

The industry was (and still is) characterized by the need to balance two things about each prospective customer: his creditworthiness and his responsiveness to a marketing offer. With greater responsiveness the cost of acquiring a customer goes down and the profitability of that customer increases. If the customer defaults on the loan, however, there is a total loss to the business. One default will wipe out the profit of many customers; so under-predicting risk can cause enormous losses. Since all customers were receiving the same deal, this meant that lower risk customers were subsidizing higher risk customers. With a good understanding of responsiveness and creditworthiness companies can avoid this cross subsidy and massively improve their economics.

However, issuers attempting to use classic target marketing faced some major problems in understanding potential prospects well enough to predict responsiveness and creditworthiness. First, they could not use questionnaires to find out the key economic drivers – customers with poor creditworthiness are unlikely to give an honest answer to the question "Do you default on your loans?" They needed behavioral information, and the information available came from credit bureaus that offered a set of common information to the credit card issuers. They summarized the creditworthiness of each individual in what was known as a FICO score, as sold by the Fair Isaac Company. These scores formed the basis of an industry wide segmentation between subprime, prime and superprime customers. An obvious complication for individual competitors was that they each had exactly the same information.

A less obvious problem with FICO scores is that they suffered from a phenomenon called adverse selection. This arose because the FICO score took no account of whether an individual would respond to an offer. This in turn meant that if someone did respond, then they were more likely to need credit (and thus be riskier) than someone with the same FICO score who did not respond. Therefore it could almost be logical to conclude that the best prospects are those who do NOT respond, which is obviously not practical. As a result the classic marketing approach had little chance of finding the fittest offers.

The answer that Capital One found to this problem was to adopt an agile approach: Information Based Strategy. By conducting a large number of tests they aimed to identify what mix of message strategy, price, credit line, product features and acquisition channel would be the most fit. Through exemplary use of TLC loops they tested numerous variants, learnt which marketing led to the best outcomes and selected that marketing variant, and then committed resources to roll it out nationally.

As a start-up, between 1989 and 1991 Capital One conducted 200 tests of different credit card offers to US consumers before identifying its first winning offer, which was a low "teaser" introductory rate of 9.9% (half the industry standard) combined with a balance transfer from a previous credit card. Where earlier tests had increased the responsiveness of customers but with a 350% increase in delinquency rates, this offer maintained the responsiveness with no increase in delinquency. So these tests helped Capital One learn things that its marketers had not known previously; the successful combinations were a surprise.

Furthermore, the competitors suffered because adverse selection now worked against them – Capital One was able to take the best customers from its competitors amongst prospects with the same FICO scores. Within three years the business grew to 5 million customers and $7bn in managed loans. This left the least attractive customers to the incumbent banks, yet they had no information to assess this in advance.

Initially the incumbents chose not to respond to the balance transfer offer, presumably because they were still making excellent returns on their credit card businesses. Of course, it was only later that the poor creditworthiness of their remaining customers would have become clear. Over time the agile approach enabled Capital One to continue adapting even as the marketplace became more competitive. Competitors eventually started copying the balance transfer offers. Then "teaser hoppers" (potential customers who shifted their balances between cards as introductory rates expired) began to destroy the economics of the balance transfer offers. Capital One was able to use its Test-and-Learn approach to identify when to exit the market. This is a good example of the importance of winnowing out offers that are no longer fit. In the mid 1990's some competitors that had claimed to have strategies similar to Capital One failed to select successfully and were forced to exit the industry.

Through further tests Capital One successfully targeted new customer segments. Often it was first to market with a successful offer, but even when it was not it could use the speed and efficiency of its testing approach to catch up with competitors who launched first.

It might seem that once the banks understood what Capital One was doing, they too could adopt the agile approach. But in fact the capabilities that Capital One developed proved to be hard to replicate.

With respect to "Test", a practical problem was that the IT infrastructure was not built both to service existing customers and to create system exceptions to run new tests. Capital One CEO, Richard Fairbank, is quoted as saying that while using the proper systems would require 2 man years to conduct one test, by using a PC and "hacking" the solution (i.e., putting together a rough-and-ready approach), the test could actually be done in a week. Requiring marketing people to sit next to the IT people and to the risk people further enhanced this capability because it helped them design tests that took into account what was actually possible.

Capital One's advantage in learning was illustrated earlier. With regard to "Commit" Capital One invested in a highly flexible and scalable system. By 1999 the company had the world's largest Oracle database and had invested in training programmers to exploit its capabilities. From the early days of hacking a PC they were now able to go from 20,000 customers in a test to a national rollout within three months, far beyond the capability of their competitors.

The final part of the jigsaw was the organizational capability and culture that Fairbank and his management team developed. They recruited the best analysts from around the world, and developed the capability to form cross-functional teams to run specific tests and projects. Their aim was "to build an organization from the ground up in which an information-based strategy was the strategic fulcrum. Where everything lined up with that vision, so that the HR systems that you use, the people that you recruit, what you pay them, how you organize, how you build the operations, the technology, the organization, everything lines up consistently with that vision."[2] The competing banks had none of this culture; their organizations were simply not set up for the Agile Marketing approach.

The scale of the difference between this Test, Learn, Commit approach and the bank subsidiaries is hard to contemplate for those who have never experienced it. One executive, who moved from a high street bank to Capital One in the UK, observed that he went from a business that conducted 7 tests during a year to one that conducted 70,000. This difference was reflected in its performance. Between its IPO in 1994 to 2000 its stock price increased 1000% and its average annual organic growth rate of 46% was the highest in the industry. More recently it has suffered in the credit crunch but it remains one of the most successful and admired financial institutions.

TESCO

Tesco, the UK grocer mentioned at the start of this book, is another business based around Test, Learn, Commit loops. The earlier story referred only to Clubcard, its loyalty card, but Agile Marketing permeates everything that Tesco does. It is also at the core of what makes it such a formidable competitor, growing from a market share of around 16% in 1995 to over 31% in 2006. Its slogan, "Every little helps" characterizes both what it offers its customers and how the business goes about delivering this.

The relative performance of Safeway and Sainsbury's on the one hand, and Tesco on the other, show both the power of Agile Marketing and its longevity.

In the early 1990's, both Safeway and Tesco were facing major challenges. Tesco most obviously was struggling to convince its shareholders that its expansion plans, funded by a rights issue, would pay off. Its market capitalization dropped to below the value prior to the rights issue (i.e., all the money stumped up by shareholders had disappeared). Safeway, created through a series of mergers, appeared to be doing well, but in reality had run out of steam and had no clear strategic view of how it would continue to grow. The two businesses had similar aims in their strategic initiatives – listen to customers and develop their businesses based on customer needs – but adopted very different approaches to undertaking the challenge.

Tesco adopted an Evolutionary Marketing approach, just as it had with Clubcard. It was first to market with initiatives such as Value line own label (to compete visibly at a low price point), Tesco Finest (a new high quality offering), Clubcard and in-store service, e.g., a "one in front" queue reduction initiative (if there were more than one customer in front of you when you queued up they would open another checkout). In each of these cases, the value propositions offered by Tesco adapted steadily over time as variants were tested, lessons learned and resources committed behind the successful offers to roll them out across the chain.

Safeway on the other hand attempted some "big bang" changes with its "Safeway 2000" project. This was a major multi year change program: Safeway planned to adjust its market positioning, launch new store formats, launch new lines of own label, restructure its store operations and build new capabilities throughout the business, as well as launching the ABC loyalty card. In each of these cases, extensive analysis was conducted first into the consumer needs, the marketplace was segmented and offers were developed for each segment. These new marketing initiatives were then to be launched to a clear timetable.

The initial results from Safeway 2000 were very positive, growing share of market and profitability, since the analysis and planning were done well. However within 2-3 years, Tesco once again had the initiative and was grabbing market share back.

The problem for Safeway was not management, nor strategy, nor execution - but rather inability to sustain the improvement or adapt to a continuously rapid changing environment, shaped by Tesco. The intention of Safeway had always been that its initial offers would be refined over time, but the amount of effort that went into launching each one, and then trying to keep up with the relentless improvements being made by Tesco, proved too challenging for the organization. Safeway seemed always to be struggling just to deliver the basics, rather than creating a distinctive market leading customer offer of its own.

By following the consensus view of good marketing, Safeway's program was a series of big bets on being right - which paid insufficient attention to the fast moving competitive environment. In particular, Safeway needed greater ability to predict the winning approach than it actually had. A particular problem was that its competitors responded in unpredictable ways to its own initiatives. Its attempts to move directly to a new marketing strategy were heroic, but impossible to be perfect in all aspects - and once set on its path Safeway could not adapt sufficiently. It found it especially hard to respond to agile competitive attacks (since it was committed to plans it could not change). In addition, Safeway could not be certain a marketing action would have the desired impact, not least because it assumed perfect execution.

But the biggest problem was that however good the analysis, it proved impossible to predict precisely how successful an offer would be. Only after consumers had chosen was there a clear measure of which offer was best.

So Safeway's strategy was always vulnerable to a fast moving adaptive approach: continual small improvements made in response to customers. It was Safeway's bad luck that this is precisely what Tesco does.

Tesco has fast Test, Learn, Commit loops for adapting its offer. These are a core part of how it is organized. For example, front-line staff are empowered to test variations in order to adapt to changes in the marketplace. It has built fast feedback loops into its way of working, not only with Clubcard, but also in the stores. This means that if a variant is not achieving its objectives, this can rapidly be identified and the variation winnowed out. Consequently, Tesco was able to conduct more pilots, test more variations and learn more quickly.

Tesco also had the necessary conditions for being able to commit to the selected variations. In particular, it was well integrated between Marketing and Buying at head office and the stores, so execution of a new idea was relatively straightforward. In addition, if the new idea needed to be adapted at a local level to respond to local conditions, the combination of good communication and local empowerment made this possible.

Tesco was therefore able to be either a first-mover or a fast-follower. It was able to shape the competitive landscape and capture first-mover advantage because it knew it could always adjust its offers rapidly in the light of initial results, as it showed with the "one in front" queuing initiative. It could also adapt to changes in the consumer landscape or to competitor activity whenever necessary, because it could rapidly sense and respond to these.

Safeway, on the other hand, did not have any of these processes well embedded into the organization. In contrast to Tesco, making change happen at Safeway was painful for its managers. They described its management processes "like wading through treacle."[3] With a lot of effort Safeway could copy an initiative such as "one in front". But while doing so, Tesco was launching new initiatives - such as Tesco Express, its new smaller format – and continuing to move ahead.

Overall, Tesco was able to create significantly greater variation in its marketing than Safeway. Consequently the detailed strategy Tesco followed was more adapted to the customer reality than Safeway.

Furthermore, there were also cultural differences that combined with these process issues to distinguish the two organizations. Customer centricity was a critical keystone of Tesco's values, whereas there was a more ambiguous shareholder and customer perspective at Safeway. This was well illustrated by the different approaches to Value lines. Tesco launched these basic own label items to provide great value to its customers, even though the margins were lower than the existing ranges. It was no surprise that Value lines rapidly took significant share of market themselves. They also, as intended, attracted customers into the shops and stopped them deserting to discount formats.

Safeway launched a similar line, but with explicit plans to avoid it being too successful, since it reduced revenue and margin on a like for like basis. The hope was that the mere presence on the shelves would give a value message, but that consumers would then buy the brands they loved anyway. Unsurprisingly, this approach was less successful.

Finally, developing a strong brand was a core part of both companies' strategies. Tesco has built a strong brand with the tagline "Every little helps". Tesco's branding efforts were successful due largely to the consistent reinforcement of the message's truth – it was always adding a little bit more that helps.

Safeway arguably had the better advertising: it featured Harry the talking baby (borrowing an idea from a popular film "Look Who's Talking" where Bruce Willis voiced the baby). This did an excellent job of communicating Safeway's family friendly approach to "Lighten the load." However, unlike Tesco who constantly had something new to strengthen the message that every little helps, Safeway rapidly ran out of news except for price promotions, which came to dominate its messaging.

Overall, although Safeway appeared to be doing satisfactorily from the outside, at least initially, internally it always seemed that Safeway was playing catch-up. Its marketers were continually surprised by some of Tesco's activities, whereas Tesco always seemed to be ready for Safeway's.

This became demoralizing and while progress was sustained for 2-3 years, eventually the effort collapsed and management sought an exit from the industry.

We will examine later this phenomenon of the sudden collapse of one competitor even though things seem from the outside to look relatively static. Von Clausewitz, the great Prussian general, once described this phenomenon as analogous to two wrestlers, who can appear frozen in one point of the ring, when one is suddenly defeated. In fact, unseen to outsiders, the winning wrestler had been continuously, almost invisibly, probing the loser's defenses. When the weak spot was found, as it inevitably would be, this rapidly led to total collapse. Safeway simply gave up when it could find no more energy to respond to Tesco's aggression.

In this chapter I examined Capital One and Tesco, two case studies of Agile Marketers that demonstrate the potential of the evolutionary approach. They provide some hints as to the principles of making Agile Marketing work, which is the topic of the next chapter. They also each show the importance of an empowered, fast moving Test-and-Learn culture, which we will explore further in Chapter 8.

NOTES

1   Capital One Financial Corporation (1998). 1997 Annual Report: McLean, VA: Capital One, p. 3.

2   Anand, B. N., Rukstad, M.G., Paige, C. H. (2000). "Capital One Financial Corp.," HBS No. 9-700-124. Boston: Harvard Business School Publishing, p. 5.

3   Personal communication. Treacle is a British thick sugar syrup like molasses.

PART 3

MAKING IT WORK

Agile Marketing implemented through Test, Learn, Commit (TLC) loops is a very different way of marketing from the traditional approach. Instead of identifying customer needs, planning how to meet those needs, and then executing against the plan, an Agile Marketer needs to try out many variants, select the right ones and commit resources of the entire organization behind the winners. There is much less emphasis on planning on the basis of previous insights. The focus is on achieving fitness in the competitive fitness landscape, while moving fast and being efficient in the use of company resources.

When seeking to develop the capability to become an Agile Marketer, I propose there are four key requirements for success:

1. **Intuition and Situation Awareness**, based on deep experience, to improve agility in decision-making and execution and avoid analysis-paralysis.
2. **Smart, scientific experimentation**, to ensure tests are conducted rapidly and cost-effectively.
3. **Behavioral market research**, to define and measure fitness accurately, to drive selection and to develop intuition.

4. **An integrated approach to execution**, "Directed Opportunism", to commit resources successfully and roll out selected variants rapidly and efficiently.

These tools and techniques combine to create a set of principles for conducting fast, efficient and fit TLC marketing. In Part 3, I examine each of them in detail and draw out the most important lessons as the "Ten Commandments of Agile Marketing."

CHAPTER 6

INTUITION AND SITUATION AWARENESS

The first requirement for success is **expert, intuitive, fact-based situation awareness.** This addresses a potential mismatch between my call to experiment much more and the need to move more rapidly. The TLC loops could be slowed down badly if every step required a slow and deliberate decision process. There are so many choices to be made: choosing which variants to create; choosing which are the fittest; choosing whether to commit to the winners or to create more variants. If every choice required detailed, specific analysis, followed by a hierarchical decision process, then an organization would continually find itself being beaten to market by its competitors.

Successful Agile Marketing requires its practitioners to know their market environment so well that most actions can be taken without a conscious decision. Studies of experts in a wide variety of operational disciplines have demonstrated that the basis of experts' success is their highly developed intuition and situation awareness, based on deep experience. Similarly, I argue that the critical need for marketers is to develop their intuition through experience, which in turn requires continual observation and assessment of the facts. They must immerse themselves in the customer experience of the product or category, to improve their understanding and feel for the marketplace in which they compete. As we shall see, they should also simplify their assessment of the facts by developing "rules of thumb" about what works.

THE CHALLENGE OF TAKING MANY DECISIONS

A major risk of the TLC approach is that it replaces a single decision (should I proceed with the marketing plan?) with many such decisions (should I commit to this variant, or to this one, or this one?). Unless these decisions can be taken rapidly, the goal of speed will immediately be defeated.

This is not news to experienced marketers. Good senior marketers in many organizations have developed an intuition about what will work in their marketplace, through immersion in the customer experience. These marketers have an accurate awareness of the market situation that enables them to interpret observations of customer behavior quickly and accurately. They know without a lot of extra analysis how a marketing activity is likely to be viewed by customers and why. This allows them to fast-track decision-making. They may also adopt rules of thumb to guide them how to respond to cues from the market place. These rules of thumb will sometimes be documented in brand books and the like, although they often remain in the heads of the senior marketers. Either way, these experienced marketers will frequently resist a more structured process that challenges their intuition, because it simply slows them down. Successful TLC marketing needs to work with and improve the intuition of these marketers, not put barriers in their way.

Academics in several disciplines have studied how people make decisions, while others have developed theories of how they ought to make them. We met *Homo economicus* earlier, who always makes decisions using the rational choice model. There is an implication in much academic decision theory that managers also make decisions according to the rational choice model.[1] According to this model they identify alternative courses of actions, weigh the pros and cons of these actions, and then choose the best one. Or at least, that is what they should do. If they don't, the theory argues that they are poor decision makers.

However, there are many studies of decision making in laboratory settings that suggest that people do not follow the rational choice model. They are therefore written-off as biased and unskilled: making numerous mistakes and failing even to be consistent in their own behavior, from the perspective of that model. Concern with this body of work has led to the new, linked disciplines of behavioral economics and behavioral finance theory.[2] These provide a valuable counterpoint to economics based on rational choice, helping to explain why markets do not act as classical economics would predict.

Furthermore, when studying experts in a more natural decision setting the evidence is overwhelming that experts in many practical fields do not make decisions in this way, yet they still achieve good outcomes. Far from being biased and unskilled, it would appear that they **are** skilled and experienced, but working to a different model. In order to explore this further, I will build on the work of two writers who focused on this phenomenon in quite distinct spheres of activity, yet arrived at consistent conclusions.

KLEIN AND THE POWER OF INTUITION

The first author is Gary Klein. He developed the "recognition-primed decision model" from his observations of experts in fields where experience counts, such as firefighting. He showed that experts typically consider just one course of action, assess whether this is likely to work and only move onto a second alternative if the first approach appears doomed to fail. They never actively make a choice between alternatives. This is in contrast to the rational choice model, which suggests that experts compare many more alternatives than novices but analyze them more rapidly, in order to make better choices.

Instead, as shown in Figure 6-1, Klein (2004) found that experts developed an intuitive skill: when faced with a situation, the experts would identify cues that let them recognize patterns that formed the basis of their understanding of the situation. These patterns in turn activated an "action script" – i.e., a possible course of action. They then used their expertise, in the form of mental models, to simulate how the action script might affect the situation and if all seemed satisfactory, would go ahead. Then the cycle started again – with the new situation generating new cues, etc. In this way, there is no risk of analysis/paralysis, because the decision step is a simple check rather than a balanced appraisal of many options against many criteria under uncertainty. However it only works for experts – novices are likely to fail at every step – see the wrong cues, recognize the wrong patterns, activate the wrong (or no) action scripts, and be unable to perform accurate mental simulations, often because they have poor mental models.

Klein's "recognition-primed decision model"

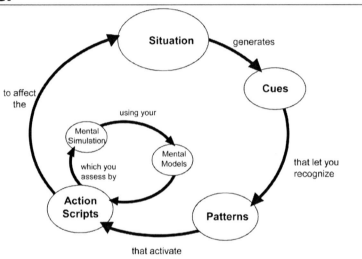

Figure 6-1

Klein has then gone on to research how experts develop their intuition and whether it can be taught to others. His conclusion, perhaps unsurprisingly, is that they have more, and more meaningful, experience to allow them to recognize patterns and build mental models. He suggests that non-experts can build up their own intuition by practicing decisions, with a focus on simulating experiences and running practice mental simulations. He also suggests that there are six barriers to developing experience and intuition in business.[3] These are

1. Barriers due to organizational structure, which can prevent people gaining the relevant experience because the task is split up unnaturally.

2. Rapid turnover of staff, meaning individuals never get much experience at one task.

3. Pace of change accelerating, leading to discounting the experience of seasoned employees.

4. Procedures (or processes) that document and describe in detail how a job should be done, reducing the opportunity for people to make regular judgment calls and gain meaningful experience (intuition cannot be reduced to process).

5. Metrics that become the aim of a decision rather than the original goal, leading to decisions based on numbers rather than the holistic situation.

6. Information technology leading to training to use the system rather than to address the situation, often leading to passive reactions to system prompts rather than gaining experience of proactive decision-making.

I think many senior marketers will recognize each of these barriers to intuition:

1. Marketing strategy and tactics are frequently separated from each other and from sales and production in large global corporations, both functionally and geographically. This prevents almost anybody gaining a broad overview of the situation and experience in how decisions in different areas interact.

2. Brand managers may stay in the same job for only a year at a time, never developing deep expertise.

3. The proliferation of new media, touchpoints and distribution channels continually leads to the claims that "it is all different now."

4. The usual solution to a lack of expertise is to document marketing processes. They are mapped, systematized and trained, without much focus on the times when these processes are not appropriate.

5. Simple metrics are put in place to achieve business goals and individual bonuses, usually with a short-term perspective. They are rarely direct measures of true "fitness".

6. Information is proliferating beyond the capacity of marketers to analyze, which is in turn leading to decision support systems in many areas of specialism. To the extent that the systems take the onus away from the marketer, they may be restricting the development of intuition.

These developments are not necessarily all bad. Indeed, to lay my cards on the table, the work I did as a consultant developing new marketing strategies and attempting to embed a more process-driven approach to marketing probably exacerbated these trends in my clients. This makes sense from the perspective of traditional marketing, since it ensures that the necessary steps are followed and analyses are conducted. It also helps less experienced marketers develop their skills in those processes rapidly. But it has probably also, regrettably, led to a loss of intuitive expertise at the heart of the marketing function.

This is a major problem for the successful implementation of Agile Marketing, which needs to be rectified. I will return to the challenges of overcoming organizational and cultural barriers to the development of intuition in Part 5. For now, we should recognize that marketers need to develop as much meaningful experience as possible. This in turn means they need to be immersed in the overall customer and marketplace experience.

> **First Commandment:
> Immerse yourself in the
> customer experience**

This will help them gain the relevant experience and work with metrics that are as close as possible to the overall goal (i.e., fitness). It will also favor processes and systems that support, rather than hinder, the development of the appropriate pattern recognition and mental models.

ENDSLEY AND SITUATION AWARENESS (SA)

The second author, Mica Endsley, has looked especially at the information technology question. Her concern is with designing systems and processes that take account of the performance needs of the users and how they can best cope with critical operations – in arenas such as aviation, nuclear power plant operation, surgical teams in hospitals or the military. She has focused on the concept of "Situation Awareness" (SA), which is defined formally as:

> The perception of elements in the environment within a volume of time and space, the comprehension of their meaning, and the projection of their status in the near future. (Endsley, 1988)[4]

Or, put more simply, "a constantly evolving picture of the surrounding environment." Being aware of what is happening around you and what that information means to you now and in the future is the basis for SA (Endsley, Bolté & Jones, 2003, p. 13).[5] Situation Awareness therefore breaks down into three separate levels:

- **Level 1: Perception** of the elements in the environment
- **Level 2: Comprehension** of the current situation
- **Level 3: Projection** of the future status

The study of Situation Awareness arose out of military thinking, in particular the causes of aviation accidents. However, although a very different application, it provides a good mental model for the marketing task of exploring a fitness landscape. The key to all marketing is first, perceiving the local environment; second, comprehending where you are on the landscape from what you observe; and third, projecting what will happen over time. With TLC marketing the challenge is to do all this rapidly - as of course it is for a pilot in a plane or the operators of a nuclear power reactor. So the theoretical research carried out in these domains can teach us some lessons for improved TLC marketing.

Good SA is the key to speeding up decisions and performance of actions. A slightly adapted version of the decision model from Endsley et al. (2003, Fig. 2.1)[6] is shown in Figure 6-2. In the main loop, Situation Awareness feeds into decision making, which in turn feeds into performance of actions, before feeding back into SA once more. This simple loop is, however, affected by the goals and objectives of the individual, as well as his mental model and the constraints of the system within which he is working. Just as in Klein's work, SA depends on mental models of how things work (made up of memory, and information processing in the brain) to go from Perception to Comprehension and then to Projection.

Endsley also points out that your Situation Awareness, combined with your goals and objectives at a given point of time, define what cues you will look for in the environment. She gives the example of an Eastern Airlines aircraft that crashed into the Florida Everglades, killing all aboard. All three crewmembers had become fixated on a problem with an indicator light and had neglected to monitor the aircraft's flight path, which had in fact been incorrectly set in the Autopilot. They simply missed the cue of where they were going due to their focus on the light.[7]

Endsley's decision model

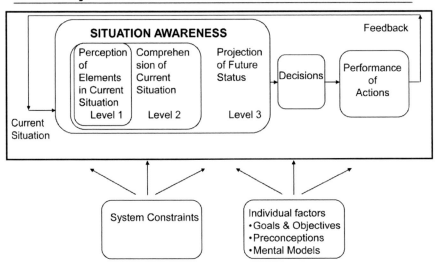

Figure 6-2

Although Endsley et al's model looks complicated; it is in fact at core very similar to Klein's. They are each elaborations of the most basic adaptive loop (Figure 6-3), which is often referred to as the OODA loop, standing for Observe, Orient, Decide, Act.

OODA is the basic adaptive loop

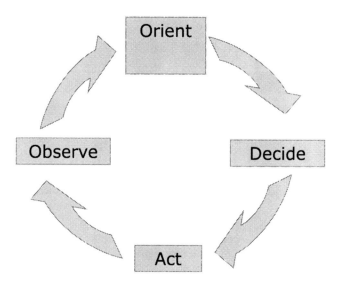

Figure 6-3

The OODA loop has just these four steps. If it is referring to a marketer, she first observes the marketplace, then orients herself to understand what her observations mean, then decides what to do, then does it, and then once again observes the marketplace after her actions. This loop can refer to experts as with Klein, to nuclear power operators as with Endsley, or to fighter pilots, which was its first use. It is also, more generally, the way creatures or organizations manage to adapt to their environments.

The concept of Situation Awareness is developed in part from the concept of Mental Models, which shows the parallels between Endsley's work and Klein's. In the language of the OODA loop, SA and mental models are both part of the "Orient" step. Endsley's proposed progression from SA to Decisions and then "Performance of Actions" is the same as the step from Orient to Decide to Act, and replaces the Action Scripts of Klein. There is however no suggestion of a drawn out approach to decisions with multiple options. Similarly to Klein, Endsley argues that good Situation Awareness permits rapid decisions moving straight onto action in critical operational roles.

In Figure 6-4 I have combined all these models into a "General Action Model." I call it an action model rather than a decision model to stress that the aim is faster actions, rather than to focus on the decision part of the loop (which most writers agree is often implicit rather than explicit).

Situation Awareness: The general action model provides a more realistic adaptive loop

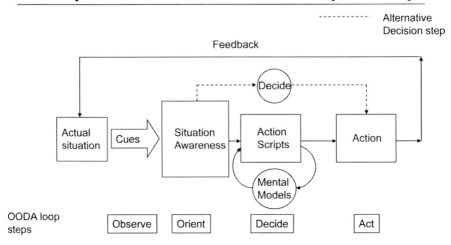

Figure 6-4

I believe that in marketing, Situation Awareness is the critical component of operationalising TLC loops so that they are fit, fast and efficient. If marketers have an accurate, evolving picture of the marketplace environment in which they are competing, they will be able to make the right choices to adapt to that environment or to shape it as they wish. SA is the mental state that enables intuitive marketing.

AVOIDING THE ENEMIES OF INTUITION AND SITUATION AWARENESS

Just like Klein, Endsley, et al., identify the enemies of SA from their experience with real-world agents.

Wrong mental models

The risk is of using incomplete or wrong analogies, perhaps through situations occurring that have not been experienced before. If the wrong mental model is applied intuition will be awry due to poor SA. This can be very insidious – Endsley et al. refer to a study of air traffic controllers that found that even very blatant cues that they were using a wrong mental model were missed 66% of the time. Instead of switching mental model, people developed far-fetched explanations to explain away these cues.

In marketing, the most likely cause of this is when a marketer with experience in one market begins work in another. Perhaps due to a belief that marketing is a generalist discipline easily transferable from one domain to another, marketers move between industries and try to apply their previous experience where it is inappropriate. Examples abound – for example, in the UK, banks and insurance companies have in recent years recruited heavily from the packaged goods industries as they sought to build their marketing capabilities. Unfortunately, this has a history of failure. As long ago as the mid 1990's the Midland Bank launched a range of current accounts aimed at slightly different customer segments. Their Marketing Director had experience of high street retail but did not understand enough about the differences between the two markets – or between the executional challenges in high street banking and in retailing. The segmented accounts were soon discontinued.

More recently, Andy Hornby, CEO of HBOS bank, having previously been a senior manager at Asda, the grocer, sought to bring a retailer's perspective to banking. In October 2008 he was forced to resign when HBOS was near bankruptcy, in large part due to the poor quality of the loans made in a period of rapid expansion. Arguably, in the mental model of a grocer he had succeeded, as sales were up significantly. Unfortunately, a marketing strategy that would have been highly successful in the transactional world of grocery appears to have had unintended consequences in the world of mortgage banking, where the true profitability of long-term contracts can only be ascertained long after the sale.[8]

Advice on improving mental models can be found both in Klein's work and Endsley's. The core need is for marketers to have deep experience and expertise in the marketplace in which they compete. Procter & Gamble is an organization that seeks to achieve this in part through a principle of promoting from within. Mars used to demand that marketers in its pet food division owned pets. Marks & Spencer sends its senior managers into the shops for two weeks every year to ensure they see their customers' experiences at first hand. Packaged goods companies used to have a "Brand Book" where all the facts about a brand were captured that could be handed onto a new brand manager to enable him to learn from the experience of others.

Second Commandment: Know the fitness landscape you are competing in

---

But in general, this focus on experience in the specific fitness landscape will be a significant challenge for marketing, a discipline that has tended to view switching between categories and companies a valuable part of career management. My argument is that this is back to front and is in fact hurting the success of marketers who move in this way. I shall return to this issue in Part 5, which discusses organization and culture.

Attention tunneling

This refers to focusing on some aspects of the environment, ignoring others that are important. The earlier example of the Eastern Airlines flight that crashed is an example of this, but there are many others. Catastrophic failures occur in all fields due to this form of blinkered vision. At a personal level, looking for a direction sign when driving can often lead to missing the cue of a red traffic light or a road user coming the other way.

In marketing, it is easy to focus on the wrong metric. For example, I worked with one food company whose product was physically heavier for the same price as a competitor. It used total tonnage of sales as the key metric, which showed it to be a strong market leader. It was blindsided by the competitor, which became the market leader in terms of value without my client even noticing for over two years – even though value was in fact the more relevant measure. Similarly, brands often have some form of brand tracking, typically assessing how their scores on key attitude metrics are performing. These metrics however are often very far removed from sales in the marketplace. I have heard marketers working for retailers and packaged goods branded manufacturers alike assure their colleagues that all is OK due to good brand metrics, while their actual market shares were in steady decline.

What seems to have happened in these situations is that once they were set targets measured by a given metric, marketers focused on achieving the target, losing sight of the original underlying goal (which was to outperform the competitor).

In a strategy presentation in 2009, Muhtar Kent, Chairman and CEO of Coca-Cola, confessed to corporate attention tunneling. "There was a period when our company did lose its way," he said. "We were too internally focused and not focused enough on the changes taking place with our consumers and customers. In essence, we were too busy looking at the dashboard and were not sufficiently paying attention to the world outside of our windshield."[9]

I believe that the antidote to this problem is to keep a true focus on fitness, not on various softer measures that relate to it. So sales is a better measure than "intention to buy," although that is itself better than "favorability" while perhaps the least useful is to achieve a "good" rating on brand image metrics. Measuring these other items may still be valuable in developing intuition and learning about the landscape, but improving them is not the actual goal.

Insufficient memory

Sometimes even experts forget a crucial piece of information in the heat of a challenging situation. This can easily be viewed as a form of human error, but often it is faulty system design that leads to this. Data overload may mean that in order to keep up with events the expert is forced to over-rely on her memory. For example it can be surprisingly hard to recall verbal instructions when driving, which means the instruction-giver has to repeat the same information over and over. In marketing, you may have to remember which promotions have been tried in which countries, which ones are unacceptable culturally where, what names are rude in which languages and such like. It is no surprise that often errors are made.

In business there is the further problem of loss of corporate memory, for example when a manager moves jobs, which makes these sorts of errors even more likely. The typical response to insufficient memory is to put in place more processes to double check for errors, but this sometimes proves self-defeating: it may add to the workload and lead directly to further errors due to stress and lack of time. A more usable approach to avoid the perils of insufficient memory is to develop rules of thumb. These can help maintain Situation Awareness by providing an easy, memorable way to move mentally from observing cues to knowing what they mean. For example, United Biscuits had a regularly updated view of the "Rules of the game" for each of its markets that helped marketers remember how to interpret cues arising in those businesses.

> ### Third Commandment:
> ### Develop rules of thumb for how to compete in your fitness landscape

Misplaced salience

Many pieces of information compete for one's attention in the world and although you may look for the relevant information your attention is likely to be distracted by the most obvious, or salient. In aircraft systems this may be lights flashing or buzzers buzzing – which if poorly designed may mean the important cues are missed. In marketing management salience is likely to be created by organizational factors – a bonus to be achieved, a boss to be appeased. If these factors are not in fact the most important ones for fitness in the marketing landscape, then situational awareness may be compromised.[10]

THE NEED FOR CHALLENGE

In short, the lesson from Endsley and Klein is that the key to speed and efficiency in TLC marketing is to develop expert intuition and to retain outstanding awareness of the market situation. This will enable marketers to stay in close touch with which offers are fit and which are not fit. This in turn requires accurate mental models built from relevant experience, clear objectives and metrics directly related to fitness, the development of rules of thumb to interpret marketplace cues and the design of organizational systems and processes that increase salience of the right cues rather than being misleading.

In order to build the capability to work in this way companies will also need to adapt their organizations, processes and performance management to support the new way of working. These organizational elements need to come together in a new "Commercial Operating System" – a concept I will define and elaborate on in Part 5.

However, even with this capability, there is still a risk that intuition will not be well aligned with the true fitness landscape for two somewhat different reasons. The first is when previously accurate Situation Awareness and intuition goes awry, which can happen if the situation has changed and the mental models are no longer appropriate. In this case experience and speed are themselves the enemy – you may simply be moving rapidly in the wrong direction. A second risk is that the marketer becomes a bit stuck in his ways and does not actively search out new ideas that could deliver new sales and profits ("We've always done it this way"). The response to both of these problems is to put in place a challenge process.

In other domains of expertise, loss of Situation Awareness is an ever present danger that needs to be guarded against – whether it is a light airplane pilot flying through fog who may literally find himself upside down without having realized it, a nuclear power operator not realizing that there has been a leak or a military commander confused by the fog of war (perhaps through some subterfuge of the enemy).

There is a significant risk of losing Situation Awareness in marketing too. For example, it can be notoriously hard to identify the turning point of a trend: daily sales figures may turn down, but extracting a new "signal" from the noise of random variation is tough. Conversely, responding to a perceived change that is not there in reality can be very costly. Another problem is that a junior marketer focusing on the responses to promotions may lose sight of the bigger picture, perhaps through attention tunneling as described above. Or he may simply not have the experience to have developed a complete mental model of the landscape.

A good solution to these problems is to institute a challenge process. This can come in two forms. First, a more senior marketer can be engaged in the assessment of the situation. This can obviously slow down the process, but in many well functioning organizations it can be part of a regular review with the marketing team's boss. Thus, a quarterly review meeting would have a specific goal of challenging the operational team's Situation Awareness, with the senior marketer asking questions about the broader picture, using her own intuition to assess where there may be weak spots.

This is how consulting firms work in their problem solving – at McKinsey a Partner will be engaged in a weekly team meeting where one of the major aims is to regroup from the activities of the past week to challenge the emerging picture of the problem being addressed. It is often surprising how easily the senior person can identify weaknesses in the working team's SA. This is NOT because they are smarter, but rather they are focusing on the broader picture and can therefore avoid the risk of attention tunneling. Equally, it is important that the organization culture permits the team to defend its views robustly in an open manner. The team on the front-line will often be correct in its assessment of the situation, since its members are closer to it.

The second solution to this problem is to take an analytical step back. Sometimes the conclusion from the challenge process will be that the landscape is different than anticipated and that the team has lost SA. Furthermore, this may mean that neither they nor the boss are confident that they can easily adjust their mental models. In that case, the return to a more determined and rigorous marketing approach may be required. Since this challenge approach is very similar to what happens when marketers have reason to believe that the standard TLC approach may not be applicable, I will discuss it further in the next chapter, which is focused on those situations.

One problem with challenging is that it is by no means foolproof. Indeed, the entire basis of TLC marketing would be far less valuable if it were, since there would be little need to explore the landscape if a senior marketer or some sound analysis could guarantee improved marketing offers. The problem, of course is that the senior marketer's intuition will sometimes be wrong, especially if she is less immersed in the market than her team. Similarly analysis, as we have seen before, is far from infallible. But this does not mean these remedies should be ignored, only that they should be undertaken with humility. By always bearing in mind the uncertainty in the fitness landscape, senior marketers can support the core team's work without assuming any sort of superiority.

NOTES

1   See for example, Keeney, R. L. & Raiffa, H. (1976). *Multiple Objectives: Preferences and Value Tradeoffs*. New York: Wiley.

2   A summary of some of the early work in this field can be found in Kahnemann, D., Slovic, P., and Tversky, A. (1982). *Judgment under Uncertainty: Heuristics and Biases.*Cambridge, MA: Cambridge University Press.

3   Klein, G. (2004). *The Power of Intuition*. New York: Crown Business.

4   Endsley, M. R. (1988). Design and evaluation for situation aware-
     ness enhancement. *Proceedings of the Human Factors Society 32nd*
     Annual Meeting (pp.97-101). Santa Monica, CA: Human Factors
     Society.

5   Endsley, M. R., Bolté B., and Jones, D. G. (2003). *Designing for*
     Situation Awareness. New York: Taylor & Francis.

6   Ibid., Figure 2.1.

7   Ibid., p. 33.

8   Of course, it is possible to move between industries, and some man-
     agers have done so successfully, but they must adjust their mental
     models significantly. Interestingly, soon after leaving HBOS Andy
     Hornby was recruited to run Alliance Boots, a retailer, where he
     appears to be having success back in his earlier area of expertise.

9   Kent, M, "Coca-Cola 2020 Vision", event for investors and analysts,
     Nov 16-17, 2009. Atlanta.

10   Some further insights into when decision makers make errors and
     possible remedies for this can be find in the book co-authored by my
     colleagues at ASMC: Finkelstein, S., Whitehead, J., and Campbell,
     A. (2008). *Think Again*. Boston: Harvard Business Press.

CHAPTER 7

SMART, SCIENTIFIC EXPERIMENTATION

The second principle of Agile Marketing is to reduce the cost and time of testing and learning through smart, scientific experimentation.

Creating numerous new variants that are mostly winnowed out through selection could be very expensive – blind Test-and-Learn might be acceptable in biological evolution, but marketers do not have the luxury of waiting centuries while unfit variants use up resources before they are selected against. We are fortunate however not to have to adopt such a wasteful approach, due to the advances that have been made in rapid experimentation in many fields over the past few years – including conducting pilots, rapid prototyping, using computer simulations and statistical data analysis such as in CRM, deploying loyalty cards and taking advantage of the flexibility afforded by digital marketing. By combining the best science of experimentation with the intuitive expertise of marketers, good experiments can be conducted more rapidly at much lower cost.

In marketing there has always been a focus on innovation – whether of products, communications, or other elements of the "4-P's". There has therefore also long been an understanding that many of these innovations need to be tested. Traditionally, products might first be assessed through market research tests, perhaps through "simulated test markets" and then trialed in real test markets in a certain geographic region. Advertising ideas may have been subject first to concept tests, then to a variety of more realistic screenings, perhaps followed again by a regional real-world test. Price changes may similarly have been tested first in customer research and then in a small-scale trial.

In most cases, however, this approach to testing is far from the TLC loops I advocate in Agile Marketing, largely because only a very small number of variants is actually tested and there is rarely any iteration following the tests. This is because a traditional piece of market research can take months and cost hundreds of thousands of pounds, while a real test market may extend the timeframe to years and cost millions. As businesses have become more concerned with efficiency, the result has been that fewer variants are tested, and then only those that are strongly expected to succeed.

In order to provide enough variety for the evolutionary algorithm to work, experimentation needs to enable far more tests using far fewer resources. There has been increasing interest in experimentation in recent years as its potential has become clear in industries such as healthcare, automotive design, semiconductors and software. For example, Steven Levitt, an economist and the author of "Freakonomics" has started teaching a course at the Booth School of the University of Chicago on "Using Experiments in Firms".

In this section, I shall first look at how traditional approaches such as piloting can support TLC loops, then explore how new technologies can enable experimentation with many more variants. Finally, I shall examine different philosophies to choosing which variants to test (statistically designed, rigorous experiments versus tests developed using intuitive judgment).

PILOTS AND PROTOTYPES

The most realistic tests can be achieved through pilots. To be effective for Agile Marketing, these must be set up rapidly and cheaply and the pilot environment must be a good match to the broader marketplace. Retailing is perhaps the easiest industry to pilot. It is relatively straightforward to run an in-market test in one or a few shops. Most elements of the offer can be tested – product assortment, in store signage, pricing, promotions, local advertising or CRM campaigns. Perhaps this ease of piloting is why Tesco is one of the most advanced Agile Marketers today. Of course, even this sort of test is not 100% accurate – there may be local peculiarities, or some unusual event may occur that is unaccounted for. But in-store tests, especially if matched against some form of control (i.e., a similar store without the test) should provide good information. In the language of evolution, this ensures the variants are selected by a sharp fitness function.

Similarly, Capital One competes in an industry where it is straightforward to measure results. By testing credit card offers through individual direct marketing, there is no contamination between the pilot and the general offer. Therefore, once again, by comparing results with appropriate controls (in this case similar consumers who do not receive the varied offer) marketers can run an experiment that provides good information about the true fitness landscape.

Another form of pilot that is frequently used is to pick a geographic region. Historically, this might have been a region of the country – for example, in the U.K. many pilots run by packaged goods companies in the 1970's and 1980's were limited to individual TV regions. The advertising that was seen in that region could be altered, while there were different retailers distributing the product with local warehouses. This meant that the pilot could be run with limited "contagion" from or to other regions. However these pilots often ran for months or even years – for example if the aim were to assess different levels of TV advertising in different regions – which is not helpful for rapid TLC loops. Furthermore, with so few regions, there were frequently several pilots being run by different competitors making it nigh on impossible to have a good control region and leaving the accuracy of the results open to doubt. However, today shorter, more rapid tests can be run. For example many grocery retailers will support pilots from their suppliers in a subset of their stores that can be set up and measured rapidly through scanner data.

A further extension of this is to use individual countries as pilots in multinational businesses. Although of course every country is different, for many global businesses their marketing offers are similar and a country can act as a pilot. In fact, major businesses such as Unilever are increasingly adopting ideas originated not in their major markets but in smaller markets. For example the advertising campaign for

Persil (known as OMO in many countries) around the theme of "Dirt is Good" was first developed in Brazil. Further developments using this idea in what Unilever calls activation campaigns (e.g., in-store displays, sports activities and public "art events") came from Turkey, South Africa and Indonesia before they were adopted in the UK. These "national pilots" cannot be as strictly controlled as a pilot store or a CRM sample. Therefore, from the view of a statistician, the data is not as good as in those cases. But in the real world of business it is possible to learn a lot from them. They certainly enable far more rapid TLC loops than if no lessons from one country are accepted elsewhere.

Software is another industry where piloting is well established, in this case through the development of prototype products. In packaged software that is resident on a home computer, different versions can be made available to different customers, whether by disc or download. This has historically been used for software testing, with "alpha" and "beta" versions of software being made available to a small number of users to test for bugs. But there is no reason why other elements of the marketing should not be tested in this way. This has become even more true for software-enabled businesses on the web, where different users can be directed to variant websites. The website may have alternative approaches to providing customer information, different promotions, varying levels of customer service, etc. Many dot com businesses use this approach to testing, while for Google it is the core of its entire marketing offer, with numerous products at any one time in beta versions. Its core technology philosophy is to launch early, aggressively review all the facts, refine, but always be 'in beta' with any product.

In each of these cases, the behavior of the customer is the main thing being measured. The most important thing is that we know whether a variant is more or less fit than others. There is no reason, however, that additional information cannot be researched. Attitudinal information to understand why a variant was more successful is invaluable in developing the intuitive feel for the fitness landscape that is critical to the overall approach. This can help improve both Comprehension and Projection (Levels 1 and 2 of Situation Awareness). This in turn means that a marketer will be better able to choose which variants to try out, which is a critical benefit of Situation Analysis.

> # Fourth Commandment:
> # Make extensive use of
> # pilots and prototypes

USING NEW TECHNOLOGIES FOR EXPERIMENTATION

Stefan Thomke (2003) of Harvard Business School[1] has examined the variety of ways new technologies can enable the sort of experimentation we require. The two main technologies Thomke describes are first, computer simulation models of real-world variants and second, combinatorial and high-throughput testing technologies. Since I believe that both of these have their place in TLC marketing, I shall describe what they mean and how they can be applied to marketing. Then I will describe a third area of technology - using the web for market research – and how that too has opened the door to faster, cheaper experiments.

Computer modeling and simulation involves representing real-world environments and objects in digital form and then simulating how they interact, all virtually. Rather than building a real-world prototype, digital versions can be created faster and more cheaply. An example Thomke describes is testing cars for their safety in car crashes. With modern day computing power it is possible to identify accurately the effect of different speeds and angles of crash on the car and its (digital) occupant. Traditional crash-test dummies in physical prototypes cost hundreds of thousands of dollars and 4 – 6 months to build and destroy; by replacing them with computer simulations, a crash could be simulated for less than $300 in just over one day (Thomke, 2003, pp. 30-36.).[2] Furthermore, engineers can conduct these experiments early in the development cycle and then run alternative variations if the results mean that modifications are required. This means that the simulated crashes have far greater impact on the final design than real crashes ever did, because the real crashes could only be conducted late in the development cycle when it was too expensive to keep making modifications.

In marketing it may be less obvious how computer modeling can help experimentation, since fitness depends on customer reaction rather than the basic laws of physics, as with car crashes. But consider the following applications:

- A new insurance website prototype can be mocked up in a few days and then tested with potential customers. There does not need to be a real life insurance underwriter behind the website – or if there does a single individual could "simulate" the entire insurance business system. This prototype can then be adapted on a daily basis in response to customer reaction, while multiple versions of the site can be tested simultaneously with different customers.

- Simulated test markets have long been a form of market testing in which consumers are exposed to new products and to their claims in an artificial forum as close as possible to the real world. They produce an early forecast of sales and/ or market share. These expensive real-world simulations are rapidly being usurped by online concept screening, where the offers are presented to members of online "Web panels" who are more easily and more cheaply reached than customers who needed to go to a hall in which the simulated test market was being run.

- One of the opportunities afforded by virtual worlds such as Second Life is to see how individuals and groups react to potential offers in a more realistic, simulated environment. Building a prototype in Second Life will take only days. At the time of writing, Second Life has fallen out of favor with marketers, but they never really tried to use it in this way: rather they sought to use Second Life as a new touchpoint for their brands or products, or to build virtual companies. Perhaps its greatest potential, however, is as an opportunity to experiment.

The second new area of technology that Thomke describes is the use of combinatorial techniques and high-throughput testing. Combinatorial techniques are now a major part of the pharmaceutical industry's approach to discovering new drugs. This combination of statistics and automation enables thousands of individual chemical compounds to be synthesized simultaneously at low cost. High-throughput automated screening then enables scientists to identify the more promising compounds for a further iteration of testing.

In marketing, the two analogous approaches to experimentation are 1) using the techniques of CRM and 2) statistically designed price experiments.

CRM marketing is based on the idea of marketing to individuals rather than to groups. By measuring and analyzing how each individual responds to different marketing offers marketers can build a picture of that individual, which can in turn be used to tailor future marketing offers to him.

This one-to-one conversation allows experimentation on many different marketing levers, which is not possible when each customer simply visits a retail outlet. Capital One's approach to piloting has brought this concept to life. The trial offers that it pilots have multiple combinations of different variables of the offer. For example, by targeting each combination at different customers it can then perform its own version of high-throughput screening to identify the most promising offers. It is noteworthy that when it does this, often the fittest combinations are a surprise to management.

This approach does not have to be based on advanced technology. For example, as long ago as the 1980's, Readers' Digest conducted similar trials with its direct mail operations, assessing for example whether a change in color of the headline offer increased take-up. Nevertheless with databases and the Internet these sorts of Test-and-Learn approaches are accessible to all. A marketer might try changing the tone of language of an offer or the benefits of the offer itself. One approach that is consistent with TLC marketing and is often used for direct marketing campaigns is the "Champion/Challenger" strategy. In this methodology, the current campaign is the "Champion" while several other possible campaigns are "Challengers". The results of each campaign are analyzed in statistically robust ways, and if one of the Challengers outperforms the Champion, it becomes the new Champion and the process is repeated.[3]

Another problem that Agile Marketers may face is some form of uncertainty that simply cannot be reduced through further analysis. Future events may be critical to the success of an offer, meaning no single estimate of the success would be valid. For example, the success of the offer could be very different if a particular competitor launches first, or if the price of some substitute product changes significantly. However, the uncertainty inherent in understanding the fitness of different offers can still be modeled using computers.

A common approach is the statistical tool of Monte Carlo simulation. This simulates a large number of "runs" of a business approach in an uncertain world. In each run, random variations are introduced and the modeled customers and other players react in different ways, according to the assumptions input into the model at the beginning. Each run then outputs a business result – when the simulation is complete there is a probability distribution of possible results. By testing the different initial offers, Monte Carlo simulation therefore allows you to assess the variability in end results, which may be of greater value than a single estimate.

The Open University has recently used Monte Carlo simulation to estimate the potential of a variety of different web-based educational offerings. The levels of uncertainty are too great to assume away – uncertainty about the number of users, of how much they might pay, of the operating costs etc., meant that single estimates of profitability carried no credibility. The interaction between these variables also meant that calculating probabilities, correlation and variances was impossible. But by simulating possible outcomes the University was able to see that only under extremely bad, and unlikely assumptions, would the offerings fail to meet their objectives. In addition they could estimate the probability of hitting a certain level of performance. As the Test-and-Learn approach proceeds they will be able to update these estimates with the actual feedback from the marketplace, thus keeping track of how actual fitness matches against the predicted fitness under which investments were made.[4]

> ## Fifth Commandment:
> ## Conduct smart experiments
> ## using new technologies

LOYALTY CARDS

Another tool for experimenting that allows rapid analysis of real-world behavior is a loyalty card. We have already discussed briefly Clubcard in the context of Tesco's overall approach to Agile Marketing. Loyalty cards have the key elements to support TLC marketing. First, the data is behavioral. Second, the data is captured and reported rapidly. Third, loyalty cards support experimentation either by tailoring offers to different customers, or by providing a precise audit of the behavior of individuals who were part of a trial (perhaps due to where or when they shopped).

In Tesco, the early use of Clubcard was as a more accurate data source of information about customers and their purchases. This allowed it to make deductions about which marketing changes might have the greatest effect. In Situation Awareness terms, existing offers were analyzed to improve perception, comprehension and projection.

An example was targeted discounting, where Tesco sought to compete with the Walmart subsidiary in the UK, Asda, which was expected to be very aggressive on price. As reported by Humby, Hunt and Phillips (2007) by analyzing Clubcard data, Tesco's marketers found that even though bananas were the single largest seller in the store, customers who were strapped for cash did not buy them proportionately. Intuitively, Tesco marketers understood that this was because the perishability of bananas made them too risky for a shopper for whom every penny counts. Cutting the price of bananas for everyone would have little effect on this segment, yet this was also the segment of customers that might be attracted to Asda. Therefore the enormous cost of cutting the price of bananas would have limited effect in addressing the Asda threat. Instead, Tesco was able to target the price cuts on more price-sensitive staple products, such as its Tesco Value brand margarine (Humby, Hunt & Phillips, 2007, p. 275).[5]

Over time the power of Clubcard data to gain a quick read on new experiments has become clearer. Not only does Tesco use the information regularly for its own experiments, it also sells the capabilities of Clubcard to its suppliers to conduct their experiments. "The Shop" is a tool that can be used by suppliers to assess how their ranges, prices and promotions are working in individual stores by customer segment (it is forbidden for privacy reasons to give information at the individual customer level to these suppliers). Some data is as recent as 10 days, which means it can be used for experiments with a very rapid turnaround. It is not disclosed exactly how suppliers are using "The Shop", and I suspect most are not yet using it for fast TLC loops, but the opportunity is there (Humby et al., 2007, p. 276).[6] Today, industry observers often name Clubcard as one of Tesco's greatest sources of sustainable competitive advantage.

Another business using loyalty cards for experiments is Harrah's, the casino operator. Since 1997 it has operated a loyalty card scheme, initially called Total Gold and since relaunched as Total Rewards. Customers can earn points for their gambling activities, such as playing the slot machines or blackjack. Originally this was used only for making typical loyalty offers such as providing discounts or the ability to redeem points for food, etc. But more recently Harrah's has used the TLC approach to experiment on offers and campaigns based on customers' individual behavior. Just like Tesco and Capital One, Harrah's conducted thousands of experiments to refine their marketing offers. By trialing multiple variants their marketers discovered, for example, that many of their target customers responded better to an offer of $60 of casino chips than to the more expensive offer of a free room, two steak meals and $30 worth of chips. They intuited that this was because their customers enjoyed the anticipation and excitement of gambling itself over the perks. This in turn enabled Harrah's to trial new variants based on this insight.[7] This is an example of how good Situation Awareness of the gambling landscape could be translated into performing better actions.

More recently, Harrah's has conducted a pilot program using the Total Rewards data in real time. It uses data to determine an individual's pain point – i.e., how much money she is willing to spend before leaving the casino. The casino uses that pain point to make marketing offers during play. When a player comes close to her limit, a staff member on the casino floor receives an alert from a dispatcher, greets the player, and offers her a free meal, a drink, or a bonus gift of money added to the loyalty card. Experiments have shown that this gift overcomes the bad experience of losing, when offered immediately. Harrah's customers then stay and play longer.[8]

DIGITAL MARKETING

A new tool that has become available to marketers in recent years is digital marketing. For many marketers, this has simply become another medium for communicating their message. It has the advantage of being measurable – e.g., through email click-throughs or actual purchase behavior from a website. Perhaps because of this, digital marketing is taking a rapidly increasing share of overall ad budgets. However, I believe that through the lens of Agile Marketing, digital marketing can transform the way marketing is done, rather than simply being another medium.

Only a few years ago, the height of digital marketing was putting a banner ad on a webpage, with the aim of enticing potential customers to click through. Then along came Google and suddenly the potential of search became clear. Although display is still an important part of the digital marketing toolkit, it now competes with search advertising in a myriad of forms. However, due to the same measurability that has attracted advertisers from the very beginning, the real opportunity in digital marketing today is to experiment. Rather than plan several months of a marketing campaign in great detail before it starts, marketers can try out some initial marketing ideas and then use the facts to refine the marketing through TLC loops.

Marketers are supported in this endeavor by Google's own strategy. Senior management at Google believes that digital marketing combines the art, science and craft of marketing every day in every decision. In terms of art, an intuitive marketer can get her ideas out into the real world fast – through different creatives (ads), targeting or offers, and see how well they work. Google encourages clients to test things online before investing heavily in other media. In particular, their AdWords auction model, which is the basis of their $5bn+ profit, allows people to run different creatives and automatically promotes the version that generates the best response. In the language of evolution, AdWords has a sharp selection function, so the quality of an initially poor campaign can very rapidly be improved through evolution.

Other technology companies are participating in the development of ever more sophisticated approaches to digital marketing. For example, Microsoft has developed the "Microsoft Tag", which allows consumers to obtain a rich media experience (e.g., an ad, a webpage, or a video) on their smart phone simply by snapping a photograph of the tag (which is basically a 2-D multicolor bar code). This is backed up by a system for marketers to tailor offers to different consumers, and to adjust the offers and media content to consumers in real time, depending on how well the initial offer performs – true Agile Marketing.

The predicted widespread adoption of RFID tags or other sorts of tags will ensure that the world of digital marketing continues to change fast. As not only Microsoft and Google, but also Yahoo, Facebook, Twitter and other companies look for ways to develop more effective advertising opportunities for clients, new TLC marketing opportunities will continue to arrive. And as more businesses develop the capability to conduct experiments in real time, the fitness, efficiency and speed of the marketing loop are all increased. Just as with biology, if this results in more rapid evolution of offers, these businesses will have real competitive advantage.

Side Box – The Evolution of Direct Marketing

Combined with Google Analytics and other proprietary analytical tools, it is now relatively straightforward for a marketer to assess the efficiency and fitness of an AdWords campaign rapidly, as well as of a broader web strategy. This obviously enables better TLC marketing, but it also has more profound implications.

Evolutionary theory applies not only to the individual marketing campaign, but also to the entire population of marketing campaigns. In other words, over time, if there were sufficient variation, a sharp selection function and the ability to replicate successful variations, we would expect all marketing campaigns to improve.[9] Digital marketing satisfies these three requirements.

First, there is a vast array of experiments being carried out – encouraged not only by Google but by all the other dot com businesses that have business models dependent upon finding a way to "monetize" the visitors to their site through some form of marketing service (i.e., nearly all of them). Second, the measurability of campaigns allows marketers to identify successful and less successful techniques, and therefore to winnow out the losers. Third, in today's connected world, successful techniques are rapidly disseminated and copied, once again enabled by the dot com companies themselves.

Due to these three aspects, digital marketing campaigns are able to evolve rapidly to greater fitness. In contrast, as I commented in the last chapter, although traditional broadcast advertising can be evaluated to some extent using, for example, econometrics, the accuracy of these evaluations is still limited. Therefore it lacks a sharp fitness function, even though the other two requirements are met. Applying the theory of evolution, the conclusion is that broadcast advertising benefits less from natural selection and is more subject to drift than digital marketing. This in turn means that although broadcast advertising may in reality be a very effective mode of marketing for a business, over time its fitness will not increase through evolution. On the other hand, digital marketing techniques would be expected to evolve rapidly, as has indeed been the case over the past decade.

Therefore, simply due to the relative sharpness of selection, digital marketing is likely to take an increasing share of the total marketing spend across industries.

Today, however, Google is currently trying to bring some of this sharp selection to TV advertising with Google TV. In an interview with Advertising Age (2009), Denis Woodside, Google's President - Americas Operations, says:

"What we're doing in the U.S. on television is very interesting, taking a layer of technology and applying it to TV to give the advertisers and agencies a level of tracking they didn't have. For example, you can put an ad through Google's TV program and test a red dress in the creative vs. a blue dress and see which commercial gets play through and which one consumers switch off. If I knew the red dress was more interesting to consumers I might think about my product development or my distribution or my inventory differently."[10]

Perhaps the new technology of digital marketing will revitalize the more traditional media and help them evolve too.

NOTES

1   Thomke, S. H. (2003). *Experimentation Matters.* Boston: HBS Press.

2   Ibid. This was in 2002. Presumably the cost of digital simulation is now far lower and the accuracy far greater.

3   See, e.g., http://www.fico.com/en/Services/BusinessAndSolution Consulting/Pages/Marketing-Services.aspx

4   For those interested in using Monte Carlo simulation in their businesses, one user-friendly program that many have used is "Crystal Ball", made by Decisioneering, now a subsidiary of Oracle.

5   Humby, C., Hunt, T., & Phillips, T. (2007) *Scoring Points* (2nd ed.). London: Kogan Page.

6   Ibid.

7   Loveman, G. (2003). Diamonds in the Data Mine. *Harvard Business Review*, May 2003, pp. 109-113.

8   Radiolab Season 5, Episode 1, *Choice* http://www.wnyc.org/shows/radiolab/episodes/2008/11/14

9   Nelson, R. R., (2005). *Technology, institutions and economic growth.* Cambridge, MA: Harvard University Press, provides a good explanation of the evolution of entire fields of disciplines.

10 Klaassen, A. (2009, April 18.) Dennis Woodside Wants to Be a Friend to Agencies, Advertisers. *Advertising Age.*

CHAPTER 8

BEHAVIORAL MARKET RESEARCH

The third principle for TLC marketing is use market research to provide more accurate selection. Behavioral market research can ensure that the Test, Learn, Commit process has a selection function that accurately reflects the true market environment. Traditional market research techniques often fail to provide this. Of particular concern are techniques that try to understand attitudes or predict behavior from "agree/disagree' type questionnaire responses, since often the customer herself does not know what she would do. In that case there is a real risk that unfit variants may be selected and evolution would not then work. However with new tools in behavioral market research it is now possible to adopt marketing metrics that are much closer to reality. Businesses are using conjoint analysis and other micro-modeling techniques, rapid-concept screening, and econometrics and other advanced statistics to analyze both experiments and real-world activity. In addition newer qualitative research techniques such as ethnographic consumer research can provide deeper insight into the motivations of customers in a real-world setting. All of these tools can support the marketer trying to improve both the fitness of her offers and her own intuitive understanding of the marketplace.

As we have seen with digital marketing (see sidebar), without a sharp selection function, marketing offers will drift rather than improve their fitness through natural selection. Good market research can also have the valuable side effect of supporting the development of Situation Awareness. It can therefore help marketers choose better variants for future tests and to interpret the results of those tests.

THE CHALLENGE OF SHARP SELECTION

Sharp selection is a major challenge in many areas of marketing, since it is often very hard to ascertain whether an offer is fit or not. Has an advertising campaign worked? Is the brand strength going to result in increased sales in the future? Has the price cut been a success or has it weakened the brand franchise? Has the CRM campaign increased the lifetime value of the target customers? If we cannot answer these questions for the trialed variants, how can we select the fittest?

This challenge is one for market research. In traditional marketing, market research plays a variety of roles: gaining insight into consumers' needs, segmenting those customers according to actionable variables, and predicting how they will react to new marketing offers. In TLC marketing, the most important task for market research is to provide a reliable answer to the simple question – "Is this variant fit?" The secondary role, however, is to provide information that can help marketers develop their Situation Awareness – in particular supporting Levels 2 and 3: Comprehension and Projection.

To answer the question of fitness, many of the commonly used tools of market research are inappropriate. For example, rather than measure attitudes or historical usage, we need to measure current behavior. Historical usage tells you almost nothing about how new variants will fare in the marketplace, while attitudes require a theoretical machinery to translate into projected behavior. Understanding attitudes can be valuable in helping the process of developing new variants, as we shall see in the next section. But the measure of fitness should not depend on the same theory. The whole point of the Test, Learn, Commit loop is for the environment to decide how fit a variant is, not pre-existing theory.

Therefore the first challenge for market research is to find metrics that are as close as possible to customer behavior in the real-world environment. It is also critical that the results can be produced very rapidly, so that the selection part of the loop does not introduce the delays in the process that we avoided earlier through the use of intuition. The ease of finding these metrics will vary from industry to industry. The importance of observing behavior rather than asking questions about attitudes can be illustrated by a study for the American Society for Microbiology, which found that 95% of people claimed to wash their hands following a trip to the bathroom. However when they actually observed the behavior of people, only 63% of people actually did wash their hands.[1]

In addition to finding the right metrics to research, market researchers can also support the marketers in deciding which experiments to run and measure. The challenge is to design the experiments in the most effective and efficient way. There are two fundamentally different philosophies to choosing which variants to test: statistically designed, rigorous experiments versus tests developed using intuitive judgment.

Marketers can learn more from a single experiment than previously by manipulating multiple variables at once. This approach to experimentation lies at the basis of Capital One's Information Based Strategy and is strongly promoted today by academics such as Thomas Davenport & Jeanne Harris in a recent book *Competing on Analytics* (2007).[2] Steven Levitt's course (with John List) on Experiments at the University of Chicago is also based on deliberately designed experiments.

The statistical method assumes the ability to control variables not under test, or at least to "block" customers together in groups where they are identically exposed to these other variables. It is based fundamentally on randomly selecting participants in these tests, to avoid any bias in how they are placed into blocks. This is the basis of the "double-blind" tests that are the core of testing for new drugs. It also assumes replicability of the tests – i.e., that the same test could be repeated to give the same result at a different time.

For some parts of the marketing mix it is natural to use statistical experimental design to choose which experiments to conduct. For example, to understand the impact of changing price on demand, the discipline of yield management (also known as price optimization) is based on statistical experimental design. Comparing the results of different customer blocks the marketer can calculate the price elasticity (i.e., how demand responds to price increases or reductions). The business can then maximize profit by using the price elasticity to assess at which price level there is the best trade-off between margin and revenue.

This approach to price management has become very common in the travel industry; both as a way of managing margins in an existing business model (e.g., American Airlines or British Air) or as a way to create a much-improved overall marketing offer (e.g., easyJet and Ryanair). Furthermore, the latter two have used the techniques not only for operational improvement but to evolve their overall offer through TLC marketing, as I would advocate.

However, I am unconvinced that the fully scientific approach is always appropriate in the rapidly changing real world of marketing. The fundamental principles underlying scientific experimentation are appropriate in the chemist's laboratory. But in business, the actions of competitors, distributors and a wide range of external factors such as the broader economy are likely to break these rules. In particular, there is rarely any chance of holding all other variables constant, nor is there much likelihood of being able to replicate the experiment under the same conditions. So the selection metric will not be nearly as accurate as the statistician might assume.

Whereas the scientific method would be to test only a few items at once and to be very thorough in exploring the effects, I believe that a more intuitive approach to testing variables is appropriate. In the language of evolution, there should be more thought in the tinkering and less randomness. The insight that the marketer brings to the experiment will be able to reduce the chance of experimenting on meaningless variables or moving in the wrong direction on the fitness landscape. That said, since unexpected results are a specific aim of the TLC method, it is important not to overly limit the possibilities – which is of course much more practicable with the advances described earlier in experimentation technology.

As we saw when discussing the general action model earlier, the mental model and goals that a marketer adopts will affect the cues she observes. Over time and with additional experience, the expert marketer will be able to improve her mental models and develop better rules of thumb for tinkering. Indeed, even if one attempted to pursue the scientific approach fully, I think the same applies. In other words there are simply so many variables that the marketer's hunch will be critical to choose where to look. In fact this is true of science too. One of the main ways in which expert scientists can do better than novices is by asking better questions. In evolutionary terms, they can use their knowledge of the fitness landscape to direct where to search for improved fitness.

As Steven Levitt has complained in his blog "The availability of experiments has trumped the asking of good questions."[3] He argues that the best economists will be those who ask the best questions, while others perform the experiments. Similarly, in marketing the key is for marketers to ask the right questions. They can use market researchers or other experts to help them answer them through experiments or other assessments.

Sixth Commandment:
Focus on asking the right questions

QUANTITATIVE RESEARCH

Measuring behavior for selection means the use of quantitative market research (i.e., research that attempts to put numbers on the phenomena being observed). Quantitative market research comes in many forms, from regular tracking of performance to ad hoc studies of particular aspects of a market. This is not the place for a detailed assessment of different techniques. However it is important to realize that there are many good market research techniques available to marketers who are looking for very rapid turnaround of behavioral measurement. These are not, however, the most frequent forms of quantitative research currently used by traditional marketers.

Some form of slow turnaround usage and attitude study is the mainstay of the ad hoc research world. However, fast turnaround research has been with us for a long time in the form of omnibus surveys (this is a survey that can deliver results in a few days, by researching a panel of pre-qualified consumers, who may be asked simple questions about a wide range of subjects on the same questionnaire). A marketer can ask the omnibus panel a few questions to gain some basic attitudinal or behavioral data. Alternatively, a more specialized panel can be recruited and trained. For example, many packaged goods companies have their own panels that are trained in specific measurements, for example food-tasting. These too allow rapid feedback on trial variants. They are, however expensive to develop and only practicable for the largest businesses.

Nowadays the potential for fast turnaround research has exploded with the creation of Web based panels, as described earlier. These panels can be used by any size of company to screen new marketing concepts. Increasingly, though, concept screening tools are being tailored to specific clients, for whom their research agencies build brand- and category-specific databases based on the "rules of the game" in those market environments. This continues to mean that larger incumbents have an advantage over newer rivals, as these tailored panels provide an outstanding foundation for rapid TLC loops.

The potential for rapid, quantitative research is only limited by the creativity of the marketer and the researcher. Although made easier by the Web, as with smart experimentation, research does not need to employ advanced technology. Some years ago Selfridges, the UK department store, was considering different locations within the building for its furniture offer. Obviously managers could track sales directly, but by following shoppers around the store, they could count how many moved between floors and between the front and back of each floor. From this data they were able to winnow out several of the proposed trial locations without needing to conduct the pilot (which would have proved very expensive for some of these locations).

More complex quantitative research comes in the form of "choice modeling." This can be especially helpful if for some reason a real-world experiment cannot be conducted. For example, Conjoint Analysis is a form of choice modeling. This market research technique analyses the trade-offs that customers make in their purchase choices. By answering a computer-based questionnaire the customer can reveal his preferences between different theoretical products or services across multiple dimensions. These results are then analyzed to build a simulation of the customers' decision processes, which can in turn be used to model how each customer would respond to new variants not even envisaged when the first questionnaire was applied. This form of computer simulation can provide insights into a broader array of marketing offers than would ever be possible in the real world – although at the cost of relying on a customer's beliefs about choices he would make, rather than his actual choices.

Another survey based research technique to increase the throughput of screening ideas comes from the use of the Web to conduct research. I earlier described how web panels have been used for concept screening. More broadly, the web has greatly lowered the cost of asking research questions, while extending the breadth of potential customers that can be reached rapidly and cheaply. This has become widely used both for consumer research and for B2B research, which historically could be prohibitively expensive. Since these surveys can be very rapidly adjusted online, many iterations of the potential marketing offer can be tried. There are now easily accessible, cheap survey tools available to anybody. Web based questionnaire tools such as "Survey Monkey" allow marketers to ask not only customers, but also other stakeholders such as their own salesmen or their distributors, about new ideas and obtain almost immediate feedback.

ECONOMETRICS

In a data rich discipline like marketing, it has long been a source of surprise to analytical types that econometrics – the application of mathematics and statistics to economic data – has not become more widely used. Sir Martin Sorrell, the CEO of WPP, one of the world's largest marketing services holding companies, is quoted as calling it the "Holy Grail" of advertising. The problem is that econometrics has not proven very useful in real-world advertising. The models that are built typically need to be adjusted in a variety of ways ("fine-tuned") in order to fit existing data. Marketers also need to provide input for a wide range of hard or impossible-to-measure variables such as pre-existing brand equity, presumed decay rates of brand equity, lead and lag time between spend and recall, as well as for the "quality of the creative." This complexity and need for subjective input have all tended to mean that econometric models of advertising have remained niche.

However, for individual companies with enough history of consistent advertising these models are in regular use. More importantly for the majority of marketers, the same techniques can be applied to other marketing activities with greater immediate impact. Pricing, promotions and sales initiatives can each be analyzed with econometric tools. Back in the 1980's I spent much of my time at Mars calculating the theoretical effect of changes in the weight of Mars and Snickers Bars on their sales in different countries. This led to a series of weight changes and "Biggest Bar Ever" campaigns. At the time I was using Nielsen data on sales in a small sample of shops, captured every two months. Today's consumer goods marketers can look at data from all shops, captured daily, to generate their models. Unsurprisingly, these models are much better than my early efforts.

These, and other, mathematical models are not as good, in most cases, as real-world experiments. But they are quick and cheap and accessible to all. At a minimum they can help marketers identify the directions on the fitness landscape to search; at their best, they can replace many experiments and save cost and time. They are an important part of the toolkit of an Agile Marketer.

Seventh Commandment:
Use behavioral quantitative market
research and econometrics to
sharpen selection

QUALITATIVE RESEARCH

In addition to quantitative research, there is also a role in Agile Marketing for qualitative market research (i.e., research that attempts to understand the qualitative factors influencing customer behavior). In particular, this can help researchers fulfill their secondary role of improving the SA of marketers.

The most pervasive form of qualitative research is the focus group. Nearly every marketer has spent evenings sitting behind a glass screen listening to her customers discuss products and ideas in a group. Given their ubiquity, it is perhaps surprising that the track record of focus groups is not good in terms of predicting the future. While focus groups are a good way of learning some basics about the fitness landscape, and the sort of language that customers use when discussing the category, they do not provide a very clear view of customer behavior or attitudes, for two primary reasons.

First, they are never intended to be statistically significant – too few customers are involved to make firm conclusions about numbers. This is why most experienced marketers would only use focus groups as a prelude to a more robust, quantitative study. Second, the group dynamic, whilst sometimes very entertaining, often means that the opinions of the quieter participants are lost.

(They can also degenerate out of control. My personal favorite focus group was a study I conducted for a wine retailer where we asked the regular users of our shop in one group to try the different wines and discuss what they thought. We watched in disbelief as they got steadily more drunk, and as they discovered that mixing red and white wine created a taste they liked and a new color that they were sure must be the way wineries created Rose. All this while the head wine buyer from the retailer was trying to explain to us that his customers had a deep understanding of the differences between the various vintages and Bordeaux chateaux!)

But while focus groups are overused, there are other forms of qualitative research that can provide enormous insights. One technique that has gained traction in recent years is ethnography. This is an approach that has developed from the social sciences of anthropology and sociology. As Harvard Management Update put it in 2001, "Margaret Mead meets Consumer Fieldwork."[4] It typically consists of observing customers and users in a real-world setting – their home or their place of business, for example. Unlike the original anthropology of primitive tribes, the techniques have been adapted from spending years observing a society, to a few hours of observation and interviews. These newer approaches are termed "Rapid assessment techniques" and have made the approach far more usable for marketers.

Ethnography as a method of research is differentiated from more traditional approaches by its emphasis on the "real world," versus more usual laboratory-based or statistical approaches such as telephone surveys or High Street interviews. In this way it is well aligned with the real-world selection requirements of Agile Marketing. It typically takes a holistic view of the user in his environment, avoiding as far as possible assumptions about how individual elements of the situation affect others. Finally, ethnographers place a premium on engaging with research subjects on their own terms and in their own context, rather than relying on the artificiality of half hour phone calls asking questions from a pre-defined questionnaire.

> # Eighth Commandment:
> ## Use qualitative research to improve your intuition

Ethnography is a good example of a market research method that can not only help identify fitness directly, through its emphasis on behavior, but that can also help build a marketer's Situation Awareness and intuition. As we saw earlier, this in turn improves the quality of future variants to be tried. As the approach matures and more people learn what can be achieved through rapid assessment techniques, it is likely to become ever more mainstream. Conversely, focus groups, which are highly artificial and give very poor insight into actual, rather than claimed, behavior, should drop in favor, at least for Agile Marketers.

NOTES

1   Mariampolski, H. (2005). *Ethnography for Marketers: A Guide to Consumer Immersion.* Thousand Oaks, CA, Sage.

2   Davenport, T. H. & Harris, J. G. (2007). *Competing on Analytics.* Boston: HBS Press.

3   Levitt, S.D., (2009, April 14). Retrieved November 30, 2010 from New York Times website: http://freakonomics.blogs.nytimes.com/2009/04/14/imbens-fires-back-at-deaton/

4   McFarland, J. (2001). Margaret Mead meets Consumer Fieldwork, *Harvard Management Update*, September, 2001.

CHAPTER 9

INTEGRATED EXECUTION – DIRECTED OPPORTUNISM

The last three chapters concentrated on ways to improve experiments and measurement of them. However, in addition, TLC loops depend on fast, fit and efficient commitment of the entire organization to roll out the successful, selected variants. This is far from straightforward. The most successful Agile Marketers, such as Tesco, are widely recognized to be excellent at execution. For most businesses, however, it is likely to put serious strain on the execution capabilities.

An integrated approach to execution across the organization is needed. Since this involves more than just the marketing department it can be quite a challenge. In fact, for most businesses the agility of TLC loops requires the commitment, typically in the form of a rollout, to be largely in the hands of the front-line that is rolling out the experiments rather than in the center. However this is often not how centralized businesses have learnt to operate.

Execution has become a major topic in business in the twenty-first century. The general belief amongst managers seems to be that if only their plans were better executed, all would be well. This is quite a change from the mid-20th century when strategy seemed to be all that mattered. In a recent survey on how strategy had been affected by the credit crunch and recession, one strategy director at a major UK company even said that strategies were felt by his peers to be something you bought from strategy consultants, whereas execution was management's job.

Personally I believe that this understates the importance of strategy. But it is undoubtedly true that good strategies need to be executed well in order to succeed. Unfortunately, most of the common approaches to execution used in practice are destined to fail. Surprisingly, this seems to be widely recognized. In a recent survey, conducted over a period of five years, a leading consulting firm collected responses from 125,000 managers from over 1,000 companies in over 50 countries. Employees in three out of five companies rated their organization 'weak' at execution.

My colleague at Ashridge Strategic Management Centre, Stephen Bungay, has been researching this problem.[1] He argues that the core of the problem of execution is the way managers have been brought up to think of managing people as similar to getting machines to do what you want. The principles of scientific management are almost a hundred years old, and were enormously valuable in enabling the creation of mass production assembly lines and the achievement of routine tasks. But marketing is not like that: there is great uncertainty in the environment, people have their own motivations and desires, and what we think will work, might not work anyway.

Taking lessons from the military thinking, Bungay suggests an alternative way to make strategy happen. The military can provide insights lacking from business because it is a field of human endeavor where plans ALWAYS go wrong. The Chief of Staff of the Prussian Army in the second half of the 19th century, Field Marshal von Moltke, developed an approach to cope with these challenges. His most famous statement from his essay "On Strategy"[2] is

> No operational plan extends with any certainty beyond the point of first contact with the enemy's main body.

This is usually quoted as "no plan survives contact with the enemy."

Common marketing thinking is that there is a gap between plan and execution that needs to be closed: basically that people don't do what they are meant to. But Bungay has identified three distinct gaps that come between plans and successful outcomes in any hierarchical or dispersed approach to planning and action. Closing the gaps requires different disciplines, but they need to constitute a coherent whole.

Bungay has shown that there are three gaps that need to be closed

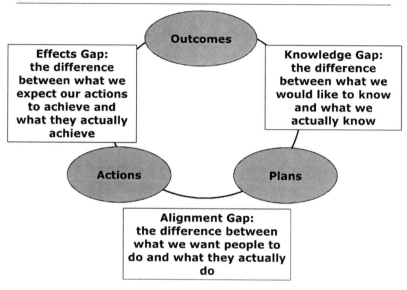

Figure 9-1

The three gaps in Figure 9-1 are between outcomes, plans and actions. The gap between outcomes and plans concerns *knowledge:* it is the difference between what you would like to know and what you actually know. It means that you cannot create perfect plans.

The gap between plans and actions concerns *alignment:* it is the difference between what you would like people to do and what they actually do. It means that even if you encourage them to switch off their brains, you cannot know enough about them to program them perfectly.

The gap between actions and outcomes concerns *effects:* it is the difference between what you hope actions will achieve and what they actually achieve. It means that you cannot predict how the environment will react to what you do.

Bungay points out that the common responses to these gaps are most likely to be ineffective. Faced with a lack of knowledge, it is intuitive to seek more information. A lack of alignment creates both top-level frustration and confusion amongst the lower levels. This in turn results in top-level managers issuing ever more detailed instructions and the lower-levels responding by delegating upwards since they are apparently not trusted to do the right thing. And faced with the wrong outcomes, top-level managers typically impose greater controls supported by an increase in metrics. However, these responses are likely to make the problem worse. Seeking more information can only slow things down. Giving more detailed instructions will not mean people are more likely to do what you want, just get busier and confused about what is truly important. The action plans increase constraints on people, creating rigidity and thus reducing agility. Imposing greater controls limits the chance for people to use their own initiative to achieve the outcomes.

Instead of these typical responses, Bungay (2011) argues for an alternative, holistic approach he calls "directed opportunism." This is itself a version of the OODA loop we have already met. Rather than ever more detailed plans leading to actions that go wrong, he argues that a fast "do-and-adapt" model is required. Specifically, in Figure 9-2 we see how this approach can address the three gaps.

Directed Opportunism

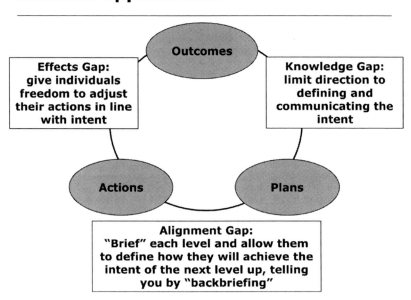

Figure 9-2

First, in the face of uncertainty the key to the knowledge gap is to think through the knowledge that is available and gather only as much further information as is needed to be able to define what really matters: the intended outcome. The direction given should make clear the intent: **what** needs to be achieved (the outcome) and **why** (the purpose served by achieving the outcome).

In the context of Evolutionary Marketing, the **why** will be answered by the results of the Test-and-Learn experiments. Marketers will need to explain clearly why the decision has been taken to commit to a particular offer. This should not be to make the case again, but to help others in the organization make sense of that they are doing.

A critical element of closing the knowledge gap is to know what is possible. With marketing, a complaint from other functions is that the Marketing department develops new ideas that are beyond the capacity of the organization to implement. Some marketers seem almost proud of their lack of understanding of the most operational elements of the business. Yet without this understanding the knowledge gap will remain.

Having worked out what matters most, you can deal with the alignment gap by making sure that this, the most important message, is passed on to others and giving them responsibility for carrying out their part in the plan. Instead of telling people what to do and how to do it, it is best to be as clear as you can about what you want people to achieve and above all tell them why; this is "briefing" them.

Then ask them to tell you what they are going to do as a result. This allows everyone to confirm that they have understood the message and have the resources to achieve it and a way of doing so within the constraints. It is best that those who are actually going to carry out the actions should do the planning. In addition, their incentives must be correctly aligned. This process is called "backbriefing."

The key elements of this approach are already present in the marketing field. They are, in fact, embedded in the way many clients brief their advertising agencies. The creative brief outlines the intent of the client – the outcome that is required, and the supporting facts to justify this. The pitch from the agency provides the opportunity to play the agency's understanding of the intent back to the client. For client/agency relationships that are working well, this combination of brief and pitch does indeed provide a flow of work that is both creative and effective.

However, too often things go awry. Sometimes the brief tries to define the media required and the key messages, as well as describing constraints arising from previous brand campaigns. In addition it is often made clear that only certain sorts of creative campaigns will be acceptable. This risks limiting the potential of the agency to apply their creativity. Sometimes the reasoning behind the brief is not sufficiently well communicated or understood by the agency. This risks them coming up with work that fits the brief but not the true intent – and thus low effectiveness.

Some clients may also argue that the alignment problem arises because the true intent of the agency is poorly aligned with the client. They suggest that there is a mismatch of incentives. For example, perhaps the client is looking for sales, whereas the agency is looking for creative awards – or worse, billings. Of course, this may be true – and certainly has been in some cases – but this lack of communication and alignment is in nobody's long term interest. This helps explain why in recent years the compensation system for agencies has been adjusted away from a percentage of the media costs and towards a mutually agreed measure of performance.

In many other elements of marketing, however, this process of closing the alignment gap is not how successful tests are copied across the business. More likely, a successful experiment is presented to operational managers as an additional initiative with limited time for briefing and backbriefing.

> **Ninth Commandment:**
> **Define and communicate the intent**
> **of new offers clearly, with a process**
> **of briefing and backbriefing**

In dealing with the effects gap, the key is to give people space and support. There is little point in trying to predict the effects that actions will have, because you can't. Instead, you need people who are ready, willing and able to use their own spontaneous, independent judgment to adjust their actions so as to achieve the intended outcomes. Rather than controlling them more, you should encourage people to adapt their actions to realize the overall intention as they observe what is actually happening. The key here is to give them boundaries that are broad enough to take decisions for themselves and act upon them. If they find that the original offer as described by marketing cannot be rolled out as proposed, they will be able to use their judgment to adapt as necessary to the internal and external environment. In fact, the best way to close the effects gap may be to move into a series of evolutionary TLC loops, driven this time by the implementing functions.

There are many potential barriers to closing the effects gap: top managers who are too authoritarian, lower-level managers unwilling to take responsibility, people of any level untrained in briefing and decision-making, an organizational structure that doesn't give the right people the right authority, or performance management systems that measure or reward the wrong thing. In Part 5 of this book I examine how a company's organization, culture and processes can be adapted to overcome these barriers.

Overall, the approach of closing the three gaps through Directed Opportunism would improve the ability of businesses to commit resources to their successful experiments. A focus on execution is critical in order to ensure that the TLC loop is completed with successful Commitment, so that new experiments can be started from the improved baseline.

> **Tenth Commandment:**
> **Give individuals in marketing and other functions freedom to adjust their actions in line with the intent**

In Part 3 we have examined how to make Agile Marketing work. In the search for speed, fitness and efficiency we identified four main principles:

- Intuition and Situation Awareness.
- Smart, scientific experimentation
- Behavioral market research
- An integrated approach to execution

By consistently applying these principles, marketers can adopt Agile Marketing without suffering from analysis-paralysis and ensure a good balance between fact-based research and intuitive insight. Through practice and experience they will be able to find their own balance between science and art.

In the course of these chapters I have identified the Ten Commandments of Agile Marketing.

1. **Immerse yourself in the customer experience**.
2. **Know the fitness landscape you are competing in.**
3. **Develop rules of thumb for how to compete in your fitness landscape.**
4. **Make extensive use of pilots and prototypes.**
5. **Conduct smart experiments using new technologies.**
6. **Focus on asking the right questions**
7. **Use behavioral quantitative market research and econometrics to sharpen selection.**
8. **Use qualitative research to improve your intuition.**
9. **Define and communicate the intent of new offers clearly, with a process of briefing and backbriefing.**
10. **Give individuals in marketing and other functions freedom to adjust their actions in line with the intent.**

NOTES

1   Bungay, S. (2011). *The Art of Action*. London: Nicholas Brealey.

2   Von Moltke, H. (1871). Über Strategie. In Grosser Generalstab (ed.), *Moltkes Militärische Werke* Bd.2, (pp. 291-3). Berlin: Kriegsgeschichtliche Abteilung.

PART 4

OTHER FORMS OF MARKETING

In the last two Parts I examined how Evolutionary Marketing, as a particular form of Agile Marketing, can allow businesses to adapt their marketing to the changing environment. I demonstrated how they are able to create major changes in the marketing offer through continuous improvement. However this does not prove that all businesses should always use Evolutionary Marketing, or even Agile Marketing.

In biology, natural selection of small genetic changes is complemented by occasional major mutations. This creates a degree of variation that often proves disastrous for the individual creature concerned, but very occasionally results in a significant improvement in the species, or even a new species. The equivalent in marketing is the traditional approach of Big Leap Marketing that we have met in earlier chapters. Sometimes, as with biology the Big Leap is required. Chapter 10 examines the implications of the need for fitness, speed and efficiency for this approach.

In competitive business, sometimes a more aggressive approach to marketing strategy may be appropriate. Rather than beat competition by developing the best offers, a marketer might instead focus on beating the competition directly – attacking their weaknesses and making it hard for them to react. There are two versions of this – Attritional Marketing, where you try to outspend your competition and beat them through superior resources, eventually wearing them down or at least ensuring higher market share indefinitely, and Maneuver Marketing, which uses the fast TLC loops of Evolutionary Marketing to outwit the competition. (Maneuver Marketing is therefore another form of Agile Marketing.)

In Chapter 11, I examine each of these forms, as well as develop a tool for choosing which type of marketing is appropriate in a given situation.

CHAPTER 10

BIG LEAP MARKETING

Am I arguing that the innovative Big Leaps that are the natural focus of traditional target, segment and position marketing, as described in Chapter 2, are never valuable? No! It is obvious that many major marketing innovations have been developed this way. In recent times P&G's Swiffer, the IBM PC, the iPod, Amazon and Starbucks have each been created through Big Leap innovations rather than continuous improvements.

In this chapter I first identify situations in which Agile Marketing is not appropriate, and what the response of marketers should then be. Just as with evolution in nature, sometimes the environment changes so rapidly that even very fast TLC loops cannot keep up. For some businesses the nature of their operations means that it is impractical to experiment with aspects of their offer, making Agile Marketing either too expensive or too slow. Alternatively, the outcome of the challenge process that I recommend as part and parcel of retaining Situation Awareness in Agile Marketing may demand a more measured approach.

I must point out that just because Agile Marketing will not work, it does not necessarily follow that Big Leap Marketing will. Big Leaps are intrinsically high risk, and the potential return may not justify that risk. I counsel you to heed the lessons of natural selection. Rather than resort to big leaps in a last desperate attempt to survive, natural selection in biology simply doomed dinosaurs to extinction. In marketing, creative destruction, as described by Schumpeter[1] and Dick Foster and Sarah Kaplan,[2] similarly suggests that a business whose environment changes too fast will fail. It is natural for a creature under threat to do all it can to survive. A business, however, does not have to. A better outcome for its stakeholders may be for it to go bankrupt or to sell itself, but the original company will be no more.

However, in many of these situations the risk-return trade-off of traditional Big Leap Marketing is attractive, if it is done well. In the second part of this chapter I argue that there are two quite different ways of going about planning a Big Leap. First there is the rigorous approach. This is what is espoused in most textbooks, trained in most marketing development programs and applied in most consultancy engagements. I call the version that I recommend the ADAM process; it consciously follows similar steps to fast loop marketing but with much more time taken for analysis and reflection.

There is, however, a second, intuitive approach to making Big Leaps that reflects how many of the most celebrated marketing innovations were arrived at, even though it is either ignored or disparaged by analytical types. I examine the pros and cons of this approach and when it might be the way forward.

Finally in this chapter I return to marketing execution. The vast majority of marketing books that focus on Big Leap Marketing are fatally flawed because they suffer from the common problem of assuming that better planning will improve execution. However, this is rarely the case. As with the Commit stage of TLC loops, a better approach is to adopt the lessons of Directed Opportunism, already applied to Agile Marketing in Chapter 9.

THE LIMITATIONS OF FAST TLC LOOPS

In the previous chapters I have argued for the potential of fast TLC loops to search the fitness landscape. But I have also acknowledged that sometimes Agile Marketing is inappropriate. Why and when is this?

There are three main types of situations when the classic segment, target and position marketing approaches are more appropriate than fast TLC loops:

- When you wish to shape the marketplace through Major innovations.
- When Agile Marketing will no longer adapt fast enough to a rapidly changing marketplace.
- When marketing experiments are too expensive or too slow.

Major innovations

In my definition of marketing I accord as much importance to shaping as to adaptation. Often Agile Marketing can shape the marketplace through the new offers that it creates. However sometimes there is an opportunity for faster and greater innovation. The literature on innovation shows that there are indeed occasions when Big Leap marketing is required – but not as many as most marketers might believe.

A good framework to explore this issue can be found in *Fast Second*,[3] a book by Constantinos Markides and Paul Geroski of the London Business School. The authors argue that there are four different types of innovation (Figure 10-1. I have added some examples of successful innovations to their framework.) They classify innovations along the two dimensions of their effect on customer habits and behaviors and their effect on established firms' capabilities and assets. I believe that for three of the types of innovation, Agile Marketing has an important role to play, but that Big Leap marketing does not. In the final type, however, it is pivotal.

If the new offer is a minor extension of the current proposition facing consumers and also builds upon the capabilities and assets of existing players in a minor way, this is an "incremental innovation." As the name implies, the challenge for marketing in this case is to deliver the best-adapted increments. This is the natural type of landscape for fast loop marketing. It is the type of innovation faced by most marketers, in most companies, most of the time.

Different Roles of Marketing

Type of innovation	Examples	Appropriate type of marketing
Incremental (Adapted consumer proposition only)	Plain Chocolate Kit Kat Innocent Drinks Dove Ford Focus	Agile
Radical (New consumer proposition and business competences)	Café in US/UK (Starbucks) Personal computer (IBM PC) Online Book store (Amazon) Download music site (iTunes)	Agile: following someone else's innovation
Strategic (Focus on new business models)	Skype Pret a Manger Smart Cars easyJet IKEA	Agile: with a new fitness function for the new market
Major (Significant new consumer proposition using existing competences)	Online Banking Post-it Notes	Big Leap

Figure 10-1

In complete contrast, "radical innovations" occur when there are major changes in customer habits and behaviors and the innovation destroys the existing industry capabilities and assets. These are the focus of "Fast Second," in which Markides and Geroski argue that first mover advantages for radical innovations have been misunderstood. They demonstrate that it is not the first company that **enters** a new market that gets the advantage (indeed they usually exit fast too) but rather the first company that **succeeds** in the market that gets these advantages and becomes the big winner. This is why I have put product categories rather than brands in the figure in the radical innovation box. None of the successful, well known brand names actually created the market: e.g., Charles Stack was first in online bookselling while Napster held sway before iTunes.

Markides and Geroski also argue that most radical innovations, such as television, the Internet, mobile phones or aspirin are supply-push innovations (i.e., they start from supply and try to create demand), not demand-pull ones at all (i.e., identifying needs and then creating products that meet them) and therefore not driven in any way by marketers. They conclude by arguing that large companies should not worry about the initial stages of "colonizing" the new market, but rather wait to be fast-second "consolidators" of the market.

The response to this work, to the extent it has filtered into the marketing arena, has been to develop recommendations of how a company and its marketing can become more entrepreneurial, more innovative, etc. But the point of "Fast Second" is that most radical innovation comes from upstarts who mostly exit the new industry soon after entering. Fast second is less sexy, but strategically smarter and much more practical to execute. So rather than use Big Leap marketing to deliver radical innovation, I am arguing that marketers should focus their attention on the incremental innovation implied in taking someone else's radical innovation and making it profitable. This is precisely when fast loop marketing comes into its own. So this situation is not appropriate for Big Leap Marketing.

The third type of innovation is "strategic innovation." Here the innovation will produce only modest changes in consumer behavior but disrupts existing competences (similar to what Clayton Christensen in his classic book, "The Innovator's Dilemma"[4] calls a "disruptive innovation"). Strategic innovations are also based largely on supply-side changes. They are based on new business designs. Since they do not come mainly from marketing changes, fast loop marketing is not the way to discover them. They need a big leap, but not one driven by marketers. In consumer terms, Skype, after all is just a new approach to delivering standard telephony; Pret a Manger, a UK premium quality fast food outlet is just a different way of delivering Marks & Spencer-style fresh sandwiches; easyJet and Southwest Airlines deliver air travel cheaper than traditional carriers.

However, strategic innovations can create new markets and shake up entire industries. Marketing will play a support role to the initial business process redesign. It must ensure that the minor changes to the customer demand are positive, or at least that negative changes are well contained. This last point is critical. Christensen examines why large companies are unable to create or even compete with "disruptive innovations." He demonstrates that these innovations typically fail the screening criteria of large companies because they do not meet the needs of existing customers. They also fail on quality hurdles, they make lower margins and they risk cannibalizing existing products.

So marketers can use Agile Marketing in these cases. There is a twist, however. They must ensure that the fitness function is appropriate for this new offer. It will be no use if the measure used penalizes the new variants for failing to meet the needs of existing customers, or having lower margins or being of lower quality. Those are precisely the features that make it possible to create the new market. Once the new business offer has been launched, just as with Radical innovations, Agile Marketing can again take the lead in modifying the offer and communicating the improvements created by the more efficient business approach. So this situation, too, is not appropriate for Big Leap marketing.

The final type of innovation is "Major innovation", where major changes for consumers are accompanied by only minor reinforcement of established firms' capabilities. Major innovations **are** marketing innovations. I have argued that often evolution can arrive at these major innovations through incremental improvement – just as evolution arrived at *Homo sapiens*. However, biological evolution sometimes requires a significant mutation to arrive at a new creature. The same is true for evolutionary marketing. So "Major innovation" to shape the marketplace is the type of innovation that demands the classic segment, target, position approach to marketing.

The challenge with Major innovations is to be sufficiently confident in the assessment of demand that the innovation will have a strong enough likelihood of succeeding. In Chapter 4, I introduced the idea of the fitness landscape and showed how evolution can be seen as a search for the highest peaks. This is a worthwhile endeavor if you cannot find the highest peaks easily by getting there directly. The evidence suggests that most businesses do not find these peaks and their innovations fail, due to some combination of misunderstanding the true opportunity or failing to execute successfully. But **if** they have sufficient insight and foresight and executional skills, then they can improve their batting average. In the second and third parts of this chapter I will give some advice about how to do this.

Agile Marketing cannot adapt fast enough

The second situation when the traditional approach needs to be followed is when Agile Marketing has been successful in adapting to the fitness landscape, but it no longer is. This can happen either because the marketplace has changed too much to adapt in time or because the challenge process suggests you have lost Situation Awareness. In either case you are stuck in a part of the landscape that is no longer fit. This is an example of what mathematicians would describe as a "local optimum."

When evolution does not work

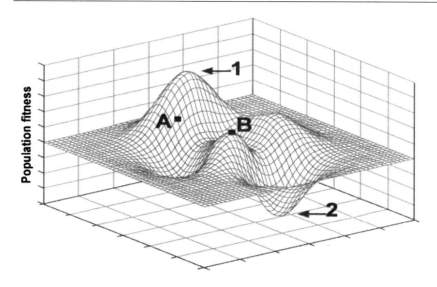

Figure 10-2

In Chapter 4, I mentioned the problem of a local optimum, as a situation when the continuous improvement approach will not reach the highest peaks of the fitness landscape. This results from the particular nature of the evolutionary algorithm and how it works in a complicated fitness landscape. Look at Figure 10-2, which is the same as Figure 4-6 earlier. Recall that, in Chapter 4, I pointed out that if a search were started at point B instead of at Point A, then there would be no small steps up from Point B. Instead, evolution would get "stuck" at point B. Point B is in fact a niche. An offer located here could win over other similar offers, but are inferior to some others in the marketplace – they will not attract resources from those higher points. This might be acceptable for a small niche player but not for a major player. The only way to escape from a "local optimum" such as Point B would be to take a big leap to escape this mound and hope to get somewhere near to Point 1. Once that has been achieved the evolutionary algorithm can be used once more to move up the slope to the top.

The marketing version of this is that the best marketing offer is very different from what you currently can offer, requiring a major innovation, not incremental development. Most importantly, as soon as the leap has been made it is critical to revert to Agile Marketing again. In this way a jump to Point A can be turned into a move towards Point 1 – hopefully fast enough to survive.

I will look in turn at the four most likely ways to find yourself in a situation where fast loop marketing cannot adapt fast enough.

1. Marketplace has changed too much

The idea of the environment changing too much for evolution to adapt is one we are all familiar with in biological evolution. Dinosaurs once ruled the world, evolving steadily, when suddenly (in geological time frames) they were gone. Similarly, in marketing, continuous improvement can cope with a lot, but not with everything.

For example, a competitor might launch a major or a radical innovation that has a significant impact on customer habits and behaviors.

If your competitor has shaped the marketplace, in order to respond in time it may be necessary to make a similarly large leap yourself. The evidence of "Fast Second" gives some encouragement here: the observation that winners in radical innovations are "fast second" means that an Agile Marketing response to someone else's supply-led innovation may be a very effective way of winning.

Markides and Geroski argue[5] that the skills required to transform an idea from a niche to a mass market include the classic marketing and sales skills. I have already mentioned Amazon, IBM, Starbucks and iTunes. Other winners who took someone else's shaping ideas include Microsoft, who did not come up with the idea of an operating system, Nintendo, who followed Atari in the videogame market, IBM whose first computer lagged Atanasoff's ABC computer, and Procter and Gamble who came up with disposable diapers after Johnson and Johnson.

Of course, the lesson of Fast Second is not that coming late to the game is a winning strategy. Being Slow Third is likely to be a losing strategy whether you adopt Agile Marketing or try to find a Big Leap.

This is also true for the second example of when the marketplace changes too fast: when the economic environment changes dramatically. Here Big Leap marketing might be the only possible response – but the risks may be too great.

I am writing this chapter during the dark days of the recession following the credit crunch of 2007-9. There is currently a shift towards value and away from luxury products in consumer markets. This is hardly surprising, but still very difficult for luxury retailers and manufacturers to respond to through continuous improvement (the best value retailers, such as Walmart, are engaging in Agile Marketing harder than ever as the marketplace comes to them). Some of them seem to be just like dinosaurs, doomed for extinction or at best, takeover. Perhaps their only chance is a marketing Big Leap, for example focusing on Asia – but the odds of success are low.

Similarly, not so long ago, the previously largest carmaker in the world, General Motors, filed for bankruptcy after years of decline, following a precipitous drop in sales of its trucks and gas-guzzling cars as oil prices surged and the economy then collapsed. I would argue that this was in part the result of its failure to adopt Agile Marketing in the past, but the same cannot be said of Toyota, which has also fallen into loss and has announced major innovations to exploit more fuel-efficient technology. The environment for carmakers is currently so changed from when they made their planning assumptions that they need to make major changes to cheaper, greener cars. Whether they can do so is still unclear. There is no doubt that a new auto industry will emerge – the challenge is whether the current carmakers will be leaders in it or not. With its own expertise at Agile Marketing and innovation I would bet on Toyota being there, probably with a fast second strategy.

2. Loss of Situation Awareness

It is less clear what the risk/return trade-off will be when the problem with fast loop marketing is a loss of Situation Awareness (SA). In Chapter 6, I introduced the idea of SA and described how to gain it and keep it. But if it is lost, then by definition intuition is no longer a sound guide and Agile Marketing becomes very risky. The only option is to take a step back and seek to reorient yourself. This means following the same steps required for a Big Leap, taking the time to analyze and reflect. Depending on the result, you may find that in fact everything is fine and you are still in a relatively fit position, or alternatively that you have gone way off track and are in serious danger. In the first case you can resume Agile Marketing; in the second a Big Leap or creative destruction beckons.

3. A competitor blocks the way

Agile Marketing is also going to face difficulties when you face a competitor that is blocking the way to improved offers. This is most likely to be the case for a smaller business facing a market leader. The market leader, especially if it has its own Agile Marketing approach, is better placed to win at all times. It starts from a fitter position, can afford to conduct more experiments, and should be able to develop better Situation Awareness. The only options for the smaller player here are either to

- Make a Big Leap and thus out-innovate the market leader. This is unlikely to succeed, for all the reasons I discussed in Chapter 4 that argued that searching the fitness landscape in the traditional way is unlikely to work.
- Find a niche to play in where the market leader does not seek to win. This can be successful, and may be achieved through fast loop marketing.
- Possibly to attack the market leader through surprise. This third, much more aggressive approach, is discussed in the next chapter under the banner of Maneuver Marketing.

4. Unable to afford the experimentation

The final reason that a Big Leap may be required is when businesses cannot afford either the cost or the time to undertake the necessary amount of experimentation. Many of my examples have come from the worlds of retailing and financial services, where it is relatively straightforward to conduct small scale experiments at low cost and to get feedback on their effectiveness very rapidly. I also showed in Chapter 7 that there are many ways to speed up and reduce the cost of experiments in other industries. Nevertheless, some firms are always going to struggle with experiments.

For example, obviously Boeing cannot afford to develop and build four different new types of jumbo and then see which one is popular. Similarly Pfizer and its fellow large pharma competitors have increasingly needed to focus resources on a small number of big blockbuster drugs, even while adopting the tools of high throughput screening in their early exploration. This is largely because regulators demand a large number of (expensive) tests on human patients during the later stages of drug development, to ensure both safety and efficacy. Here too, experimenting with numerous drugs, even if they were all safe, would be enormously costly (this phase can cost hundred of millions of dollars for each chemical formulation that undergoes human trials).

It is also possible that conducting the experiments would itself create a problem by eliminating the potential for surprise. For example, it was suggested to me by a manager in an electricity company that although he was interested in the impact of changing the price of power, if he were to trial a new price competitors would see it and negate the opportunity. This may indeed be a problem in some regulated industries, but it is usually quite easy to keep small-scale experiments secret, through the tools of telephone outbound calling or direct mail offers. And even if the experiments **are** observed by competitors, if there are sufficient variations, as I would recommend, it is most unlikely that a third party could deduce anything from it except that price was being examined. In fact, far from removing the potential for surprise, as I discuss in Chapter 11 it is possible to exploit rapid TLC loops to disorient your competition and then surprise them with your initiatives.

Putting it together

From the preceding sections, it should be apparent that there is no absolute rule as to whether fast loops or Big Leaps are appropriate. Rather situations lie on a spectrum (Figure 10-3). The nature of the industry matters, but equally the specific marketing lever being considered also matters.

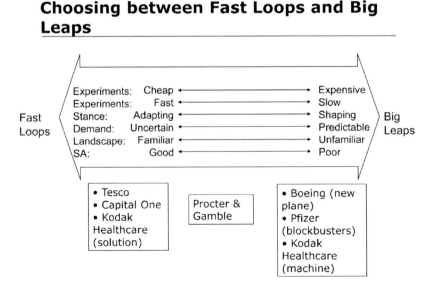

Choosing between Fast Loops and Big Leaps

	Fast Loops		Big Leaps
Experiments:	Cheap	← →	Expensive
Experiments:	Fast	← →	Slow
Stance:	Adapting	← →	Shaping
Demand:	Uncertain	← →	Predictable
Landscape:	Familiar	← →	Unfamiliar
SA:	Good	← →	Poor

- Tesco
- Capital One
- Kodak Healthcare (solution)

Procter & Gamble

- Boeing (new plane)
- Pfizer (blockbusters)
- Kodak Healthcare (machine)

Figure 10-3

The main dimensions underlying these choices are:

- Whether experiments can be carried out both cheaply and rapidly, which would support fast loops, or whether experimentation is expensive and slow which would necessitate Big Leaps
- Whether your strategic stance is to adapt to the environment, where fast loops would be valuable, or to shape the environment, which may require a Big Leap
- Whether demand is uncertain, where fast loops will be more beneficial, or predictable, in which case the risk of a Big Leap is reduced
- Whether you are familiar with the landscape in which you are competing, in which case you may be able to search the landscape through fast loops successfully, or if it is unfamiliar, in which case you may be forced into larger, blinder leaps
- Whether you have good Situation Awareness to support rapid TLC loops, or if you lack Situation Awareness making TLC loops more risky and Big Leaps relatively more attractive.

For example, if a company can conduct numerous trials cheaply it will have greater success with the evolutionary approach, whereas if it can only afford one option, it is forced into a larger leap.

It is when these different criteria result in different answers that difficult choices have to be made. For example, if you were a small player in a rapidly moving technology industry, you would face a different trade-off. You might be able to launch cheap experiments rapidly and intend to adapt to the environment, all of which favors fast loops. Yet you would also find demand unpredictable, the landscape unfamiliar and in general have very poor Situation Awareness. These last three elements militate against successful fast loop marketing, possibly forcing you into Big Leaps, which nevertheless would be very risky. This illustrates the fact that the position on this spectrum will be affected both by the industry in which you compete and also your starting position in the fitness landscape. If you are far from the peaks today you are far less likely to know exactly where fitness lies than if you are the market leader. So laggards are often forced into larger leaps than industry leaders, with the consequent risk involved.

Even in a fast moving industry such as grocery retailing, Big Leaps are appropriate for some decisions. Tesco may have no difficulty using Evolutionary Marketing for pricing and ranging, but it is a different matter when developing a new superstore format. Its current position is due in part to a Big Leap it took in 1993, using a share rights issue to fund a major push into larger properties. This nearly went disastrously wrong, as Big Leaps sometimes do, but once they had understood the new landscape, the then Marketing Director, Terry Leahy, was able to lead the business upwards through fast loop marketing under the banner "Every little helps".

There are also businesses that lie in the middle of the spectrum. Differences in consumer landscapes will result in differences in how companies search for market share within them. Procter & Gamble (P&G) mixes Big Leaps with fast loops. Packaged goods manufacturers play in a less complex, less rapidly moving consumer landscape than Tesco, as there is a slower pace of innovation and competitors do not move so fast. We would therefore expect managers to have a better idea of what innovations consumers may buy and thus be more willing to leap. We would also expect to see larger investments in each innovation from P&G than from Tesco as a matter of economic logic because of an expectation of higher payback. This is both because P&G is taking a less risky bet in innovating, due to its greater confidence that it can find an attractive spot and because it can expect to make profit from the innovation for longer, since it expects the innovation to stay attractive for a significant length of time.

The evidence shows that P&G does indeed invest far more resources in R&D for larger scale product innovation than Tesco - and is far more successful in these launches than most of its competitors. It has been very creative in finding these innovations. For example, it is leading the way in Open Innovation. This is the philosophy that good ideas may come from anywhere, and are indeed unlikely to originate from within the closed walls of a single company. By working with outside inventors and bringing its own marketing and distribution skills to bear, P&G has been able to identify more promising new markets. It is effectively creating major innovation by piggybacking on these inventors with a "Fast Second" type approach. Successful new products introduced this way include Swiffer Dusters, Crest SpinBrush, Olay SK-II Regenerist, Mr. Clean Magic Eraser and Glad Press'n Seal.

Nevertheless, it is still very hard to predict success in advance - something like 80-90% of packaged goods innovations fail. Part of P&G's success in its industry is that it has been more successful in these innovations than its competitors. Once a new product has been launched and had initial success, Procter then seeks to add it to its list of very highly successful products (i.e., those selling over $1bn worldwide) for decade after decade. The way it does this is, however, in part quite similar to Tesco's, in making continual small adjustments to its marketing mix, looking at new segments to target, incremental innovations, etc. By continually adapting innovations over time, as well as adjusting them internationally, it turns promising Big Leaps into well-adapted offers for the local consumer landscape.

P&G is also always seeking to be at the forefront of innovating in marketing tactics. From the days when it produced its own "soap operas" on TV to attract audiences large enough to receive its promotional messages, to its leading role today in developing new modes of marketing using the Internet, Procter devotes time and effort to seeking out new marketing tactics. Here too it combines a Big Leap with the thoughtful tinkering of TLC loops.

Side Box: Intelligent Design (ID): Big Leaps in Marketing

You are no doubt familiar with the arguments between those who believe that man is the product of an evolutionary process of natural selection and those who argue that we are the result of intelligent design.

Just as evolution stands in contrast to intelligent design in the theory of Creation, so Evolutionary Marketing stands in opposition to traditional marketing. With Evolutionary Marketing nobody knows where the continuous improvement may take the offer. In traditional marketing a new offer is planned as the result of segmentation, targeting and positioning - a form of intelligent design. Of course there are differences between the biological and marketing version of each as outlined in this table, but the essence of TLC loops is very different from that of segmenting, targeting and positioning.

This points to one of the advantages of Evolutionary Marketing. For intelligent design to work, the Designer needs to be omnipotent, omniscient and infallible. Indeed, these characteristics are the point of the Creationists' argument. However, the dominant form of marketing in most industries is traditional marketing, in spite of the fallibility of the human agents. In other words a marketing innovation is planned and then executed, in spite of the lack of either omniscience or omnipotence, each of which is critical if you are to be confident of success in an uncertain changing, competitive world. So making Big Leaps through the traditional approach is a high risk/high return activity, based on the closest the marketer can get to the perfection of omniscience and omnipotence.

	Pure Evolution	Evolutionary marketing -TLC loops	ID in Marketing - STP	ID in religion
Agent	None	Human - fallible	Human - fallible	Omni-scient
Mindset	None	Lots of testing, a bit of thinking	Lots of thinking, a bit of testing	?
Variation	Lots of random variation	Lots of thoughtful tinkering	Best efforts design of a single offer	None required
Selection	Survival of the fittest	Survival of the fittest during testing	Survival in the market place	Created perfect
Replication	Reproduc-tion of survivors	Amplification through agile execution	Executional excellence	Omni-potent
Efficiency	Most wasteful	Many failures	Highly efficient if successful, else very poor: High risk, high return	Not relevant
Value of speed	Evolve more rapidly and enhance overall population fitness	Enhance fitness by meeting customer needs and defeating competitors	Trade off speed for acuity in understanding competitors and thinking	Not needed: omni-science and omni-potence

HOW TO MAKE BIG LEAPS WORK

There are two basic approaches mere humans can adopt to improve their success with Big Leaps. The first is based on rigor in marketing planning and the second on intuitive creativity.

Rigor in marketing planning: the ADAM process

Several authors have written about ways to develop rigorous marketing plans. There are recommended approaches in most of the textbooks, including Kotler and Keller.[6] Marketing courses at business schools outline the steps, tools and frameworks required. Within industry, clearly defined marketing processes provide the foundation of how more sophisticated marketing departments and consultancies go about their jobs. These approaches have formed the basis of their marketing training process. Diageo, the alcoholic drinks company, has spoken in public about its "Diageo Way of Building Brands" (DWBB) process.[7] Unilever has developed a similar way of developing marketing plans that it calls the "BrandKey".

The approach I recommend for adding rigor to marketing is what I call the "ADAM" process. ADAM stands for Analyze, Decide, Act, Measure (Figure 10-4).

ADAM - the rigorous approach to Big Leaps

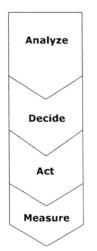

Analyze
- Consumer trends
- Customer segments
- Competitor position
- Brand positioning
- Market opportunities

Decide
- Product attributes
- Marketing strategy
- Brand plan
- Go-to-market approach

Act
- Execute marketing tactics
- Launch new product
- Manage cross-functionally
- Conduct CRM programs

Measure
- Ad hoc Market research
- Tracking research
- Sales results
- Market share

Figure 10-4

Let's look at these steps one at a time. Analysis is where the traditional disciplines of market research can be applied. It is when the opportunity to develop deep insights into customers and demand must be grasped. Customer trends can be analyzed through desk research and sales results. New customer segments may be found through ad hoc market research. These analyses can help to develop greater understanding of where competitors have relative strengths and weaknesses. Brand analyses can assess where the emotional attributes of different brands appeal to customers and the extent to which the brands might be stretched or be repositioned. All of these elements can then be brought together in a point of view of where there are market opportunities to be grasped.

In the Decide phase, the analysis needs to be turned into a plan. From the insights already developed, the marketer can select the product attributes that will be the core to a better offer than competition can provide. That then leads onto developing a marketing strategy to support the product offer, including the 4P's and, if appropriate, a branding approach. The go-to-market approach (i.e., how the offer is brought to market through distribution outlets and sales approaches) is also planned at this stage, seeking to ensure availability of the chosen marketing offer to the target customers.

Once the plan is in place, the marketer needs to Act. The marketing tactics that are controlled by the marketing department need to be undertaken efficiently and effectively, in conjunction with marketing agencies. If a new product is to be launched it must be done flawlessly as planned (unlike most new launches where the plan is not followed, as described in Chapter 3). In particular, the cross-functional requirements of the marketing plan must be well supported. Similarly if there are CRM tactics planned, they too require systems and processes to function smoothly throughout the campaign. I will discuss this in greater detail later in this chapter since I believe that acting is the stage where Big Leaps often go wrong.

Finally, and critically, the results of the program must be measured. This will require a combination of ad hoc research to understand how the program is received by the target market against the chosen objectives and dedicated tracking surveys, sales analyses and assessments of market share. The measurement is important because it will lead on to the next stage of the marketing program – which will be the continuous improvement of evolutionary marketing.

This is not a fundamentally new planning approach, nor am I trying to suggest that the processes developed by others are wrong. I have tried to synthesize these processes and combine them with best practices that I have observed. The main reason I propose ADAM is that it is very clearly analogous to the fast loop marketing processes of TLC marketing. You can see this most easily by mapping ADAM onto the general action model introduced in Chapter 4, as in Figure 10-5.

The differences between ADAM and TLC marketing, apart from the obvious fact that the ADAM process is not a loop but a one-off are:

1. ADAM tries to enable you to develop insight into the marketplace and foresight into how it may change. TLC loops, on the other hand, adapt without requiring this insight/foresight.
2. ADAM replaces the automatic response of action scripts and mental models with a formal decision process.
3. The ADAM process therefore has only one chance to get it right, whereas TLC reduces the risk by allowing frequent adaptation and course correction.
4. To manage the increased risk, each step of ADAM must be conducted rigorously and with sufficient time for analysis and reflection, which makes it a much slower process, very demanding of marketing management's time.

Execution is equally important in both cases, requiring both good communication between decision maker and implementer, and accuracy in implementation.

ADAM maps onto the general action model but "Decide" replaces existing action scripts and mental models

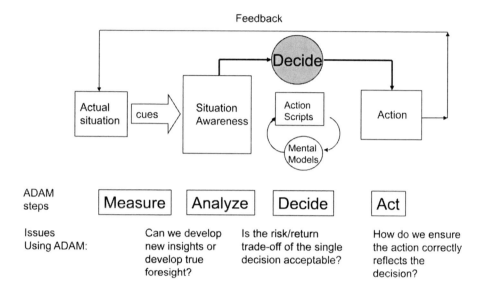

Figure 10-5

The insight/foresight developed through this classic approach to marketing allows management to confirm or revise its overall understanding of the marketplace. In the language of Agile Marketing, this in turn resets the Situation Awareness. If appropriate, marketers can then develop new rules of thumb. This in turn provides the critical precondition for successful TLC loops.

In short, as I observed earlier, the main challenge following a Big Leap is to adapt rapidly to the new environment that you have leapt to. Adopting the rigorous but slow ADAM process can provide the foundation for a new series of rapid TLC loops to meet this challenge.

As a consultant, I am usually brought in when top management believes that there is something wrong with the marketing (typically due to bottom line results). Since there is no way I would have good Situation Awareness (just like the transplants from other industries with the wrong mental models described in the previous section, it would be dangerous to rely overly on my potentially misleading previous experience) I always follow the ADAM approach. It is striking how often this provides genuine new insights to the incumbent management, even though the steps themselves are not especially difficult. That simply demonstrates the potential value of this process. It is equally striking that there is much less value in doing this a second time – a good marketing team is able to work with the new picture of the landscape quite successfully.

Just Do It – an alternative approach to Big Leaps

ADAM provides a rigorous way to develop insight/foresight and then to exploit it. Big Leaps, planned rigorously, can allow businesses to transform their prospects in the marketplace. But some marketers make major leaps without adopting the rigor of ADAM.

The examples in Chapter 4 of Akio Morita of Sony and Steve Jobs of Apple arguing against market research exemplify this. Morita launched the original Walkman on a belief that the Walkman would find a market. Steve Jobs of Apple apparently commits resources based on his instinct about what people want from their technology. This has led to a transformation of Apple's fortunes and the creation of a series of winning concepts, in particular, starting with the iMac and Mac Book computers, but more dramatically the iPod, iTunes and the iPhone.

In retailing, I have held Tesco up as a poster child for fast loop marketing. In the same industry in the UK, however, Sir Philip Green is a very successful billionaire retail entrepreneur. He is famous for a hands-on management style: walking around his shops and identifying opportunities to lay out merchandise better, problems with clothing styles, customer service problems and the like. He has also made a number of major acquisitions. It is hard to imagine Sir Philip at any stage using the full rigor of an ADAM process. He is using his intuition, just like the experts we discussed in Chapter 6 that were studied by Klein. However he is not following an experimental TLC process, simply making changes and moving on.

You may be reading this section and thinking – "Surely these intuitive Big Leap successes are a strong argument against using either TLC loops or the ADAM process. After all, if these undoubted successes use neither approach, why should I?" My answer is that by examining only successes we get a very misleading view of the risks being run by conducting intuitive Big Leaps. In fact, insight and foresight are often illusory, as our failure to predict events demonstrates.

The collapse of some of the world's largest banks has demonstrated that even the smartest people can misjudge risk horribly. A recent book from the field of finance examines very low probability events. N.N. Taleb calls his book "The Black Swan"[8] because these events can happen even after many, many occasions of them not happening – just as black swans were first seen after everyone had concluded that all swans were white on the basis of only having seen white swans. In financial theory, black swans are very important in spite of being rare, because they can dominate the overall results from history.

This unpredictability pervades life and business, causing persistent failure in spite of all best efforts. We have all seen statistics suggesting that around 8 out of 10 line extensions fail. In biology, 99.99% of all biological species that have ever existed are extinct. In business 10% of all companies in the US disappear each year. We know that smaller companies fail more often, so you might assume that perhaps big companies survive. Unfortunately not! In 2001 my colleagues at McKinsey, Dick Foster and Sarah Kaplan wrote in "Creative Destruction" that of the first list of top 100 companies formed in the US in 1917, by 1987 61 had ceased to exist; 21 still existed but were no longer in the top 100; and only 2 of them outperformed the overall market in share performance.

Black swans can be either good or bad: the greatest successes may be as unpredictable as the greatest failures. I believe that many major innovations are unpredictable black swans – or at least, unpredictable by us. Even innovations such as Amazon and Starbucks, while easily explainable after the event, were arguably black swans that could not be accurately predicted beforehand. Why do I say this, when presumably Jeff Bezos of Amazon and Howard Schulz of Starbucks would argue they had a clear view of why and how they would succeed? Because at the same time as they were developing, countless retail propositions and dot com companies set up shop and have never been heard of again. Many of their founders also believed they had a clear view of why and how they would succeed.

In reality, it is very hard to distinguish luck from skill in Big Leaps. However, the very high levels of failure in innovation and the low Return on Investment (ROI) on much marketing investment suggest that successful "just doing it" depends more on luck than judgment.

If this is true, then you should not keep trying to predict the unpredictable by intuitively aiming for a few, major innovations. The problem with all this research in strategy, finance and economics is that it appears quite fatalistic – most things fail, so you will fail too. The response of most managers and consultants is, perhaps unsurprisingly, to produce prescriptions of how not to fail. Managers and consultants are by nature optimists. That is probably why they engage in their work every day: waiting for a black swan to wipe them out might not inspire them to great effort! But being optimistic does not guarantee success.

In fact, there is a significant risk that recommendations on how to improve innovation are the result of business delusions. As demonstrated in a recent book by Phil Rosenzweig, *The Halo Effect* (2007),[9] so-called successes may not be as great as they are believed to be, there may be luck more than judgment involved, and they may even suffer from logical flaws.

Rosenzweig describes some common business delusions that affect judgments on innovation. The following list takes some of his and combines others.

- *The halo effect.* One of the most pervasive delusions in business is the halo effect – when a company does very well, people conclude that everything about that company is fantastic – the leader, the people, the strategy, the culture, its execution, etc. So commentators immediately view as uniformly excellent a company that launches a successful innovation.

And the same company a few years later, when its performance dips, is terrible at everything – awful leader, processes
that did not adapt to the new reality, sclerotic culture, unable
to execute in the new world. Enron is the classic example.
Today, there is an undoubted halo effect around Apple and
Steve Jobs.

- *Confusing luck with skill.* A second error that I fear is often
present in discussions of innovation is confusing luck with
skill. This is very easily done. To illustrate, imagine, as did
Daniel Dennett (1995, pp. 179-180),[10] a leading philosopher
of mind, that there were an international coin tossing competition. Each county needs an entrant. The UK might well
decide to be absolutely sure it had the best possible entrant
for this prestigious prize. We could have a grand elimination
tournament; with everyone entered into a straightforward
knockout, best of three tosses wins. Simple calculation shows
that this tournament would only need 26 rounds for every
citizen to enter, probably organized geographically. It could
become a "Britain has Talent" reality TV show.

    By Round 24 (the quarter finals) we would have the best
8 coin tossers in the country. Their techniques would be analyzed, their training examined, their mental attitudes and
preparation regimes put under a microscope. A theory of best
practice would emerge, and over the following 3 weeks, these
would be refined until the British Champion was crowned.
Perhaps he or she would have a clear view of what led to victory. Certainly the winner would feel very special. And they
would be special – after the fact. They DID win. But of course
it was just luck. They were not actually any better; their techniques, training and mental preparation mattered not at all.
And they are no more likely to win the international tournament than someone eliminated in the first round.

    We have already seen that there is a big chunk of luck involved
in innovation, so how can we know that a successful company has

been skillful as opposed to lucky? We see a company that has successfully innovated and we conclude that it is a great company (no doubt influenced by the halo effect). But we cannot be sure it has not been lucky – any more than seeing a lottery winner allows us to conclude they are great at picking tickets.

- *Connecting the winning dots.* Another problem with much discussion on innovation is that the analysis looks only at the winners. But if you only look at the winners, you are falling into a logical trap. The advice we are giving managers is of the form "If you do THIS, then you will be successful at innovating." But the advice is only valid if it distinguishes successes from failures. We need also to have demonstrated that "If you fail at innovating, you will NOT have done this." We must examine failures and how they differ from successes, with facts that are not sullied by the halo effect, before making conclusions.

- *Applying lessons from one domain into another.* A last logical error is to assume that because something improves innovativeness for one company, it will improve it for others. What works in packaged goods manufacturing may not have much relevance for computer makers (where the role of technology may be much higher). What works in grocery retailing may not have much relevance in packaged goods manufacturing (because the ease of experimentation in retailing is so much higher). What works for a challenger may not have much relevance for a market leader. Good science pays a lot of attention to categories – trying to group observations into categories that differ on critical dimensions. In studying innovation we must take the same care.

To summarize, there are many reasons to be skeptical about the claims of most of those who intuitively make Big Leaps. Nevertheless, some people genuinely DO seem to have the knack. Steve Jobs has turned around the fortunes of Apple with a string of Big Leaps that confound the statistics. Sir Philip Green has grown his fortune throughout the retail business cycle in ways that suggest more than a random gamble. I cannot discount the possibility that continually making intuitive Big Leaps is a valid business approach. But the simple fact that everyone comes up with the same names suggests that others are not going to be able to adopt this successfully for long.

A similar situation can be found in the field of investment management. Here the data is much more easily available than in business, so the risk/return equations can be analyzed. The efficient market hypothesis (EMH), widely taught in business schools, implies that attempting to beat the market by picking stocks is doomed to failure. The facts seem to back this up, since most investment managers do not beat the market, certainly not after subtracting their own costs. The majority of managers who had a strong run reverted to average performance, or were shown to be taking much greater risks. This in turn has led to the growth of tracker funds, which only aim to be average, at much lower cost.

But in fact, this logic falls foul of a mirror image of connecting the winning dots. There could be other reasons than the EMH for fund managers' mediocre performance. On the other hand, Warren Buffett has consistently beaten the market, for far longer than probability would allow and even after his basic investment approach was sufficiently well known to be copied. Buffett's success does show that it IS possible to beat the market, and thus disproves the EMH. So too does the existence of investment bubbles, which suddenly collapse without new market information being known. But even though the EMH may be false, the fact remains that almost no one else manages to outperform, so it remains sound advice not to try this yourself.

You may be able to "Just do it" and intuitively achieve a Big Leap.

But if you need to succeed, my advice is to adopt the rigor of ADAM unless you have the wisdom of Jobs.

Implementing Marketing Big Leaps

The fundamentals of the ADAM process are taking decisions based on insight and foresight and then acting on them. So implementation is critical here, as it is with TLC loops. Stephen Bungay's three gaps, (Figure 10-6) as discussed in the last chapter, are equally applicable to Big Leaps. Indeed the gaps are in many ways likely to be larger than with rapid TLC loops.

Bungay has shown that there are three gaps that need to be closed

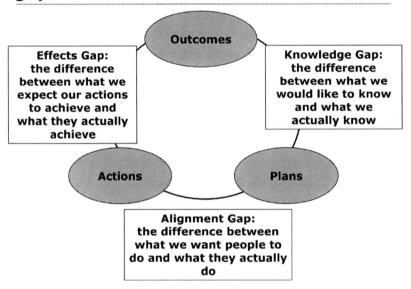

Figure 10-6

We have tried to close the knowledge gap through the analysis prior to decision-making, but there are bound to be many remaining uncertainties. The alignment gap may be large because by the very nature of a Big Leap we are asking people to do things they have never done before, which they may be doubtful of. The effects gap may be especially large, since the new actions may not have the effect we expected.

Focusing on the effects gap, if you are making a Big Leap because TLC loops are impractical, creative problem solving is key to closing the effects gap. When the outcomes are not what we were expecting, the people who will act are best placed to develop and execute new ideas. The development of ads or other communications following the creative brief process does exactly this. The intent is clear and more creative approaches to achieve it are positively encouraged: generally clients are encouraged to support distinctive or uncomfortable ideas, so long as they are well targeted at the intent.

However, broader marketing initiatives too often struggle with the effects gap. The front line in a bank rarely has the freedom or capabilities to "adjust the plan in the face of contact with the customer," to adapt von Moltke's adage (although some bank staff do seem to treat customers as the enemy).

B2B marketers who develop a solutions strategy are likely to find that the customer service reps do not deliver initially against the plans, not least because the logistics, customers and competition are all somewhat unpredictable. The question is whether they are sufficiently well trained to adapt their actions to the observed reality.

These insights about the gaps can be relatively straightforwardly translated to the ADAM process.

- **Analyze** only what really matters. Reduce the knowledge gap by focusing on insight into the current environment (consumers, competitors and trends) and foresight into how it will change, but do not get too hung up on detail.
- **Decide** the overall marketing intent, but allow marketing teams, salesmen and marketing agencies to define how they will achieve this intent. Brief them clearly on what and why this is what you are trying to achieve, and have them brief you on their proposed actions, so you can be sure they have understood the intent and the resource constraints. Encourage them to be creative in their responses. Ensure their incentives are aligned with yours.
- **Act** through the front line. Do not expect to close the effects gap simply by demanding greater effort or instituting a hire and fire policy. Instead, provide support and resources, trusting your people to adjust their actions in line with what they

see happening to achieve the marketing intent. Back creative solutions.

- **Measure** against the strategic intent with a focus on market share and profit, rather than inappropriate KPI's based on detailed plans and out of date criteria. If the execution approach encourages initiative to achieve the intent, then measuring against the intent is all that is required.

This approach to execution should be adopted in all marketing activities. However, after each campaign, it is critical to follow the example of the military and debrief on what worked and what didn't. You must learn the lessons from what is working and not working to prepare better for the future and to transfer best practice. If individuals have not performed, now is the time to understand why and decide on actions. If the strategic intent was wrong, different lessons must be learned.

In this chapter I examined when more traditional "Big Leap" marketing may be needed to complement fast TLC loops. We saw this might be the case for three main reasons:

1. When you wish to shape the marketplace through an innovation,
2. When fast loop marketing will no longer adapt fast enough,
3. When marketing experiments are too expensive or too slow.

I then introduced the ADAM process as a rigorous, thoughtful approach to conducting a Big Leap, drawing on the lessons of traditional marketers, academics and consultants. This approach of analyzing, deciding, acting and measuring mirrors the approach of TLC loops. However ADAM has no experimentation and is much slower, putting the focus on purposeful decisions rather than adaptive experiments. I also examined the "Just do it" approach to intuitive Big Leaps, arguing that it is far less likely to succeed than most managers and books would suggest. Nevertheless, the occasional maverick does seem to have the gift to do this.

Finally, I showed how Bungay's theory of planning and the three gaps could apply to Big Leaps and the different steps of the ADAM process. This combination of ADAM and planning should improve the hit rate of Big Leaps, while following them with rapid TLC loops should improve the process still further.

So I have now examined two different but complementary ways to adapt your marketing to the local market environment. The question now is – are there other approaches to marketing to have in your toolkit? This is the topic of Chapter 11.

NOTES

1   Schumpeter, J. A. (1942). *Capitalism, Socialism and Democracy*. New York: Harper & Row, 1976.

2   Foster, R. & Kaplan, S. (2001). *Creative Destruction*. New York: Doubleday.

3   Markides, C. C. & Geroski, P. A. (2005). *Fast Second*. San Francisco: Jossey-Bass.

4   Christensen, C. M. (1997). *The Innovator's Dilemma*. Boston: HBS Press.

5   Markides & Geroski, *Fast Second*, pp. 67 – 86.

6   Kotler, P. and Keller, K. L. (2009). *Marketing Management* (13th ed.) Upper Saddle River: Prentice Hall.

7   See for example, Malcolm, R. "100% Marketing", The Brands Lecture, June 17, 2003. London: The British Brands Group.

8   Taleb, N. N. (2007). *The Black Swan.* New York: Random House.

9   Rosenzweig, R. (2007). *The Halo Effect … and the Eight Other Business Delusions That Deceive Managers.* New York: Free Press.

10   Dennett, D. C. (1995). *Darwin's Dangerous Idea.* New York: Simon & Schuster.

CHAPTER 11

MANEUVER AND ATTRITIONAL MARKETING

In the previous chapters I have discussed both Evolutionary Marketing and Big Leap Marketing. In Chapter 4, I outlined how to use the fast TLC loops of Evolutionary marketing to adapt marketing offers to the customer and competitive landscape. I used insights from evolution and natural selection to explain why fast TLC loops can successfully sustain adaptation in a changing environment. I also showed that the same approach could be used to shape that environment by influencing customer expectations.

In Part 3, I examined the principles of fast loop marketing and developed Ten Commandments for marketers to follow in order to become more agile. Then in Chapter 10, I examined when the more traditional approach of Big Leap marketing might be required, arguing that this might be when the opportunity or need to shape the environment rapidly meant that it was the only option available, even if the company were inherently agile. Alternatively it might be when the company was unable to be sufficiently agile for evolutionary marketing, when fast loop marketing could not adapt fast enough or marketing experiments were too expensive or slow.

Both Evolutionary and Big Leap marketing focus on looking for the best solution for the customer. The strategic stance is therefore on shaping or adapting to demand rather than directly attacking competition. These two approaches to marketing therefore focus on the first two elements of my definition of marketing:

- *Shaping the market environment through innovation*
- *Adapting to changes in the environment*

In this chapter, I will discuss two types of marketing that are primarily focused on the third element of the marketing definition:

- *Beating competition*

The idea of directly focusing on beating competition can be applied in several situations – for example if you are a market leader facing smaller innovative new entrants, conversely if you are a small company facing a larger competitor, or if you are conducting a specific marketing and sales campaign aiming to convert customers from a competitor.

I have previously borrowed some lessons from military theory, but when considering a strategic stance that focuses on beating competition, the military is even more directly relevant. (There is the critical difference that in marketing, competition is conducted through the medium of the customer, which introduces a complexity not present in warfare - except perhaps in the battle for Hearts and Minds. Nevertheless, actively targeting a competitor is a different stance from focusing all energies on improving the customer offer.)

Traditionally, marketers have adopted what I call Attritional Marketing to defeat competition. By outspending their competition they have increased customer awareness and distribution and kept competitors at bay, even when their fundamental customer offer might be less attractive. This has parallels to attritional warfare, as we shall see, where simply having more people and ammunition allows the larger army to defeat the smaller one.

Exponents of Evolutionary Marketing have an alternative option, however. They have developed an organizational capability to be far more agile in their marketing than competitors that follow traditional marketing planning approaches. Up to now, I have described how they can use this agility to drive a Test-and-Learn approach, through low cost, rapid experimentation. However, there is a more aggressive way to use the same skills that minimizes the amount of testing. Changing the marketing offer very rapidly has tremendous potential to generate competitive advantage. The key is not only to react to the existing competitive environment, but also actively to seek to create and take advantage of weaknesses of your competitors, to confuse them or even demoralize them, so that they do not take the appropriate actions to remain in the competitive battle. I call this approach "Maneuver Marketing."

In this chapter I will first examine how the military has developed and applied the ideas of fast adaptation to maneuver warfare and how that contrasts with more traditional attritional warfare. I will then expand on the idea that much traditional marketing is in fact attritional and not directly focused on the customer, and assess some of the advantages and disadvantages of the approach. Finally, I will describe Maneuver Marketing, the application of fast loop marketing to beating competition. I will discuss its similarities to maneuver warfare, and develop a framework to help businesses assess which form of marketing to adopt when.

MANEUVER WARFARE

It may be a surprise for me to suggest that the military could provide a good example of agile competitiveness. After all, the essence of TLC marketing is for marketers to follow their intuition with very limited control from above, yet the military is typically viewed as the ultimate command and control organization. However, as demonstrated by Field Marshal Von Moltke and Stephen Bungay in the approach to execution discussed in earlier chapters, the story is not so simple. Following orders is still central to the military culture, but increasingly there is recognition that to complete missions on the front line, the combatants need to have the ability to adapt what they do to the current situation.

Von Moltke followed a tradition of thought inspired by the writings of Von Clausewitz,[1] although similar ideas are also apparent in the ancient Chinese writings of Sun Tzu.[2] This work led to a new way of working in the Prussian military, which in turn led to the adoption of new military tactics known by the term "Blitzkrieg." There is also a well-known book on Marketing Warfare by Al Ries and Jack Trout (1986)[3] that refers to Von Clausewitz when proposing how to adopt a competitive approach to marketing. However, the most relevant work for understanding the application of fast adaptation to military thinking is the work of Colonel John Boyd.

John Boyd was a very successful fighter pilot who later transformed the way the US and other countries fight battles through his theories. His work is best remembered in the development of the OODA loop, which we have already met in Chapter 4 as the simplest version of the adaptive loop. The OODA loop (Observe – Orient - Decide – Act) is a description of the decision cycle, be it of a fighter pilot, or a battalion commander. The most common depiction of the loop is shown in Figure 11-1 (which is the same as Figure 6-3).

OODA is the basic adaptive loop

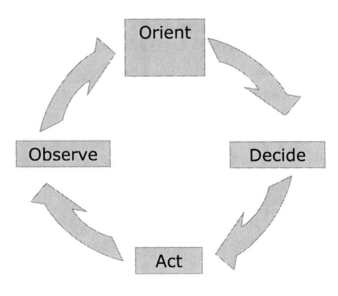

Figure 11-1

Several strategy thinkers have referred to the OODA loop. For example, Stalk & Hout (1990, pp. 180-184))[4] mentioned it when outlining the elements of time-based competition, as did Tom Peters (1987)[5] when discussing how to adapt to a rapidly changing environment. A more detailed examination of how Boyd's strategy work can be applied to business is by Chet Richards, in his 2004 book "Certain to Win."[6] These authors use the OODA loop to describe how an organization or an individual can adapt more rapidly to a changing environment, or indeed use speed to surprise the competition or even shape the environment in its own favor.

Boyd's fundamental interest was in beating the enemy, not in adapting to the environment. His core idea was that with a more rapid decision cycle than your competitors you could outmaneuver them, even when they had greater resources than you. You would then have the ability to respond faster, AND increasingly to confuse your competition as to what is happening. The final element of maneuver warfare, once you have surprised the competitor and exposed a weakness, is to commit resources to exploiting that weakness and achieve the commander's intent.

Maneuver warfare was introduced as an alternative to attritional warfare. Throughout history, military commanders have sought to have greater resources, in terms of manpower and/or weaponry, than their enemies. Simple arithmetic says that if you have 20% more resources than the enemy and if you lose resources at the same rate, then when you have lost half your resources they will have only 30% left and you will have nearly a 2 to 1 advantage. If that is not enough, after another halving of your resources, you will have 25% of your original resources and the enemy will be down to 5% - a 5 to 1 advantage.

Attritional warfare can be very effective. It is, however, inherently wasteful of resources. This is particularly problematic in modern-day democracies when it comes to human life, but that problem has been partly addressed by refocusing resources on weaponry. Now, of course, the cost of new technologies and weapons is also a political problem in most democracies.

More worrying for the attritional warriors is that maneuver warfare appears to give the smaller army some good opportunities for victory. At its most basic, maneuver is an approach to warfare that stands in contrast to attrition: winning through agility and surprise rather than through overwhelming force. In practice all battles have an element of both, but the main purpose of maneuver is to dislocate the opponent using speed and surprise, and the purpose of attrition is to overwhelm the opponent by means of physical destruction. To put it simply, you can win by being clever or by being strong. Of course, being strong and clever is best, but is not an option available to all.

Boyd approaches the challenge of agility by introducing the concept of "working inside the decision cycle" of the enemy. This is most easily understood in the original context of a fighter pilot and using the four stages of the OODA loop.

1. The pilot initially Observes something – say a blip on the radar.
2. He then needs to Orient himself – understand where he is, where the enemy is, and indeed if the other blip is an enemy at all.
3. Then he Decides what to do, say carry on for now in the same direction.
4. Then he Acts – i.e., carries on.
5. Then in a second go round the OODA loop, he then Observes what happens.
6. If the blip acts aggressively, the new Orientation will be that it is an enemy plane.
7. Our hero may then Decide to engage in a dogfight
8. He Acts by veering in a new direction.

Going round this loop over and over again, it is clear that this follows the principles we discussed earlier of TLC marketing. In particular it is critical to move round the cycle fast: a pilot who did nothing while analyzing the situation for 5 minutes would certainly be dead, however good his analysis and subsequent plan.

But there is more to it than this. If the pilot is operating inside the decision cycle of the enemy, it means the enemy may still be trying to orient itself even while our pilot is moving onto the next action. The enemy will always be trying to react to his actions, while struggling to keep up. This will inevitably result in it rapidly getting into a very weak position. For example, if the enemy has just worked out that our pilot has "zigged", when he has in fact gone round the cycle one more time and "zagged", he will have surprised the enemy, which is the key to winning a dogfight.

This ability to surprise through speed is at the core of Boyd's thinking. It is this element that Stalk and Hout (1990) picked up on in describing time-based competition. "A time-compressed company does the same thing as a pilot in an OODA Loop … it's the competitor who acts on information faster who is in the best position to win."(p. 180).

Boyd takes it even further, arguing that in a military action, continually doing this will sap the morale of the enemy soldiers until, so confused and unable to react to your latest move, they give up trying, and succumb to rapid defeat. This can happen even if they have superior resources in terms of manpower and weaponry.

The simple loop above, however, as used in most management texts, misses some of Boyd's most important points, as is pointed out by Richards (2004, p. 65).[7]

Boyd emphasizes that Orientation is the key. If you are well oriented, then you do not need to go through a specific decision step, your actions are implicitly guided by the orientation. Thus an experienced fighter pilot knows what to do when he sees something and can act more quickly. This explains the fact from the Battle of Britain that those pilots that made it through the first week were then much more likely to survive until the end of the war – they had learned from very tough experience (Bungay, 2000, p. 373).[8] As with Klein and the recognition-primed decision model, orientation not only leads to action but also to which mental models you adopt and which cues you notice. The parallels between orientation in this context and Situation Awareness described in Chapter 3 should be clear.

Boyd also proposes that the primary importance of the Test-and-Learn cycle is to develop orientation (or Situation Awareness in my language). You need to test new hypotheses when what you observe does not quite fit your orientation or when you have an idea that could lead to new insights. This Test-and-Learn cycle interacts with the changing environment and with any other new observations to adjust your orientation and thus help you adapt your actions.

In terms of my general action model, the OODA loop when applied to maneuver warfare suggests that the explicit Test-and-Learn cycle is an occasional luxury to build capability, rather than the main loop to adopt in the heat of battle. The most important element is speed, achieved through intuitive Situation Awareness. These ideas form the basis of maneuver warfare, as practiced by many of today's modern armies. They have led to rapid victories in many cases, from the defeat of the French by the Prussians at Sedan in 1870, through the German victory over France in the Second World War, to more recent conflicts including the First Gulf War.

COMPETITIVE MARKETING

What can we learn regarding competitive marketing from the military? I think the two main insights are:

1. Attritional Marketing is as dominant in the marketing world as Attritional warfare once was in the military.
2. Using agility to beat competitors through Maneuver Marketing has great potential, both strategic and tactical.

Attritional Marketing

I believe that the vast majority of marketing today is attritional. After a big leap innovation, marketers settle down to spending resources to beat competitors in key battlegrounds – often looking to achieve greater awareness, but also spending on sales to achieve higher distribution, or promoting to achieve lower prices in the short term. Little of this is really an attempt to adapt to the environment or to shape customer demand. It is an attempt to beat competitors. Of course marketers can only beat competitors through attracting customer spend, but there are clear parallels to attritional warfare.

This helps explain why the most important metric to most marketers is their marketing budget. It goes almost without saying in marketing circles that someone with a larger budget is a more successful or senior marketer than someone with a smaller one. Marketing CV's always boast about the size of the budget the marketer has controlled. Budget planning discussions are usually phrased in terms of the increase in resources that is required to achieve the goals.

For those with the resources, there is little doubt that Attritional Marketing has been effective. By outspending on advertising and promotions (above and below the line, in marketing speak) and with larger sales forces, market leaders have been able to maintain a competitive advantage, often with products that are no better than the competition. The long-term success of major brands in packaged goods, even in light of competition with own label brands of equal product quality, is evidence of the success of this approach.

However Attritional Marketing is rarely efficient, I believe, and the focus on spending more has probably led not only to many of the complaints from other functions that marketing is wasteful, but also to similar problems in procurement of marketing services such as advertising that the military faces in procurement of weapons (when the amount you spend is a positive, there is little incentive to save costs).

Equally worryingly for the vast majority of marketers is that if they are not market leaders they have little chance of winning an Attritional Marketing battle and remain profitable. The same arithmetic applies here as in the military. With net profit margins before advertising and promotion of, say, 20%, if the market leader spends 10% of sales on marketing, a player half the size would eliminate all its profit trying to compete.

Finally, as with the military, if a more agile mode of competition can allow smaller, nimbler competitors to beat lumbering giants, then attritional warfare will no longer even be effective.

Maneuver Marketing Basics

In earlier chapters I described how to use agility to adapt better to the market environment through Evolutionary Marketing. The insight from Boyd is that there may be an alternative use of agility: using it to surprise and then defeat less nimble, possibly larger competitors.

There is evidence from the commercial world that competing against an agile competitor does indeed cause all the problems identified by Boyd. An example is the one discussed at the end of Chapter 5, when examining the competition between Tesco and Safeway. As described, Safeway found itself putting more and more of its efforts into reacting to initiatives from Tesco. Because customers were already expecting these improvements, every effort was an attempt to meet basic requirements rather than to create Safeway's own future. Its managers felt that every day was a vain struggle not to be quite as much worse than Tesco as the day before. Yet every time Safeway's managers felt that they had made progress, Tesco surprised them with some new initiative already well under way to implementation that moved the game on further. It seemed that Safeway could never win: management was always chasing yesterday's initiative. This became very dispiriting. It was in that context that merger discussions started with various parties and, eventually, that management threw in the towel and recommended being taken over by Morrison's.

Adopting the insights of maneuver warfare to marketing means using rapid TLC loops to drive aggressive competitive activity. The aim is to surprise competitors and then to attack them at their weakest point with all the force that you can muster.

This differs from Evolutionary Marketing due to the difference in objective. Rather than iterating through multiple Test-and-Learn loops before committing to successful offers, Maneuver Marketers will choose an offer that their experience and intuition says will be a good one, commit to it and then as soon as they are able to observe the market impact, make adjustments. The speed of change will be hard for competitors to observe and respond to in time, before the Maneuver Marketer has moved on.

Since there is no time to experiment before committing, choosing the variation is similar to the approach adopted by the expert firemen in Klein's work – a mental simulation is all that will be possible before an action script is activated. This should be adequate, since the key to success is not that the variation is itself an immediate winner. Rather, it begins to shape the market place and to cause the competitor to respond to what you have done, rather than have time herself to step back to test and learn. The power of this is that as you move around the loop to create new offers, customers come to expect what you can offer them rather than what your competitor used to offer them. This in turn creates an urgent need for a competitive reaction – a need they may be unable to meet if you are going round the loop too fast for them – "inside their decision cycle".

I believe that Maneuver Marketing can be used both as a strategic approach and as a tactical approach.

Strategic Maneuver Marketing

The strategic opportunity is for a smaller business or new entrant to attack a market leader who is less agile. In this case Maneuver Marketing is adopted because the opponent has superior resources whereas the smaller company has a capability advantage in its agility. In analogy to warfare, it is clever but not strong

I propose two alternative versions of strategic Maneuver Marketing.

In the first version, the aim is purely to attack the competition as cleverly as possible, without attempting to improve the marketing offer to the target customer. In the second version, agility **is** put to use to improve the customer offer, but focusing resources on where the leader's offer is weak, aiming to steal share rapidly.

The first of these is manifestly not a customer centric approach – it is using time to mess up the competition rather than improve the lot of the customer. There are not many clear examples of this, but one that arguably follows the maneuver approach is Ryanair. Originally developed as a European version of Southwest Airlines, Ryanair has grown into the third largest airline in Europe. It developed a rigorously low-cost business system, learning lessons from other low-cost airlines and adding in many new ideas of its own. In light of its growth and financial success, it is perhaps surprising that it was also viewed as the least favorite airline by TripAdvisor each year from 2006-2009, and that it consistently receives criticism from consumer bodies for its customer service.

At the time of writing (May, 2009), Ryanair has been in the news in just the past week for the following stories: supposed plans to charge customers for using the toilet in their planes; imposing a charge for online check-in at the same time as increasing the cost of airport check-in (with a plan to eliminate check-in desks entirely); producing misleading and insulting advertising; unacceptable credit-card charges; misleading pricing information on its website; and asking passengers to take their bags to the plane themselves. Equally, Ryanair has been the first to allow mobile phones on some of their planes (as yet not receiving complaints from people annoyed by this) and they are consistently the cheapest flights to a given location, even after the hidden charges. It must also be stressed that many of the stories may have no or little basis in fact. But this is the nature of Maneuver Marketing – rapid shift in focus providing minimal opportunity for competition to respond before the story has moved on.

One of Ryanair's major competitors has been British Airways (BA) on its short haul routes. Battling with the legacy costs of its days of public ownership, not only is BA unable to match Ryanair on costs, but also unable to keep changing its tactics and processes anywhere near as rapidly as Ryanair. Each of Ryanair's new areas for complaint is eliminating something that BA sells as a benefit. It would appear that many customers do not value the benefit enough, yet BA cannot respond. Each new idea from Ryanair must cause surprise in the ranks of BA (the toilet story certainly did). From a customer perspective it appears that BA has simply given up trying to compete with Ryanair on short-haul flights (after earlier attempts to respond such as launching its own low cost airline, Go) and instead retreated to focus on long-haul, business class passengers, just as would have been predicted by Boyd.

Ryanair's CEO, Michael O'Leary has been quoted as saying: "The more we can sound nasty, petty and cheap, the more we can reinforce in people's minds that we are extremely bloody cheap, and they will choose to fly with us" (Handley, 2010).[9] As an aggressive approach to maneuver marketing it seems to be working. BA has lost 38% market capitalization in the past 5 years whilst Ryanair has gained 93%.

But why do I argue that this approach is not focused on the customer: surely low prices are a customer-focused value? My response is that while that may be true, other elements of the strategy are harder to justify as benefiting the customer. For example, the advertising that Ryanair does is generally accepted to be controversial on purpose so that it can generate additional publicity. This approach meant many complaints were made to the regulatory body for advertising in the U.K. (The Advertising Standards Authority: ASA). In April 2008, the ASA referred the airline to the overall industry watchdog, the Office of Fair Trading (OFT) for persistently breaching its rules on misleading advertising.

Between April 2008 and May 2009 the ASA received 121 further complaints about Ryanair, but the regulator referred these to the OFT. The latter added the complaints to its file, and in July 2009 Ryanair agreed to increase the clarity and transparency of its website and other advertising. Yet in January 2010 the CEO of the OFT described yet another new initiative of Ryanair as "puerile", suggesting that Ryanair had not entirely reformed in the eye of the regulator! As the marketing press observed, by continuing to use its own agility Ryanair has beaten the regulatory system for years, "effectively giving the airline carte blanche with its advertising".[10] It is hard to argue, however, that this has been in the customers' best interest.

An example of the more customer-centric version of strategic Maneuver Marketing can be seen in the behavior of Virgin Atlantic in its own competition with BA, this time on long-haul flights (which is where, as we noted, BA has increasingly retreated). Although equally agile in its marketing strategy, in contrast to Ryanair, Virgin's strategy has been to provide levels of customer service and price that BA cannot match. When reporting results in May 2009, at the height of the credit crunch and consequent recession, Virgin Atlantic reported profits of £68.4m, an increase of almost 100% from the previous year, while BA subsided to its greatest loss ever of over £400m. The accompanying press release observed, "Throughout the last financial year, Virgin Atlantic continued to scoop many key awards for its products and services. Its flagship Heathrow Clubhouse has won several awards for being

Best Airline Business Lounge; Skytrax and Business Traveller named the airline's Premium Economy cabin as the best in the air; while Virgin Atlantic was also chosen as the Best Scheduled Airline to the US at the Travel Weekly Globe Awards". It also managed to take a sideswipe in the same press release at BA's plans to combine with American Airlines.

One target customer segment for Virgin Atlantic has been younger business class passengers who were not wedded to the traditional national flag carrier. Virgin's goal was customer acquisition from BA. An early initiative pioneered by Virgin Atlantic was having flat beds in their Upper Class, which effectively gave a key First Class benefit for Business Class prices, at a time when BA could not have rapidly upgraded its business class seats, taking several years before they matched Virgin. Similarly when BA made a big deal of recruiting mature experienced air hostesses for the exemplary customer service they could deliver, Virgin hired attractive younger women, used them in its advertising, and let the mostly male, younger target customer decide which he preferred. Virgin was also first to provide outstanding business class lounges, massages on planes, ice creams on overnight flights and a raft of other minor initiatives that allowed their communications to play up their young, agile nature compared to the more staid and slow moving BA.

Both the founder of Virgin Atlantic, Richard Branson and Michael O'Leary are masters of Public Relations, picking minor initiatives to trumpet their respective airlines, while BA seems to be in continual public arguments with its unions (even though privately Ryanair staff are said to be very unhappy, very little public evidence of this is ever provided). BA is in the uncomfortable position for a full service airline of having had strikes for the past three summers, disrupting their service to holidaymakers. Naturally, both Virgin and Ryanair have made the most of this in their communications.

By its very nature, there is no simple rulebook for successful strategic Maneuver Marketing. However, the lesson from Virgin suggests one approach would be:

- First, choose a well-defined market segment to target, where you believe the competitor is weak and where you have good Situation Awareness allowing you to move round the cycle fast.
- Second, pursue a goal to capture market share rapidly from the competitor (most often acquiring new customers, although in some markets it might be sufficient to increase share of wallet from existing customers).
- Third, commit resources to attacking the competitor's weakness with the target segment, based on initial results from the effort. In particular, follow up initial share gains with more aggressive moves.
- Fourth, use marketing communications and Public Relations to trumpet your efforts and talk down the competitor in order to shape the public debate and increase the momentum of the shift in share.

Tactical Maneuver Marketing

The second, more tactical version of Maneuver Marketing is when developing a specific marketing campaign. In this case there is very limited opportunity to test and learn during the campaign, so rapid TLC loops demand the best insight and intuition marketers have to date. But since most campaigns do have a very clear competitive goal, Maneuver Marketing can be adopted to maximize the impact of the campaign.

This approach has been adopted by at least one marketing consultancy, vSente, which has published much of its thinking online.[11] There are few well-documented versions of these sorts of aggressive marketing tactics, although they must in fact occur all the time in all sorts of situations. The challenge with them is to keep up the pressure – adopting Maneuver Marketing tactics is not the same as making one very aggressive competitive move – e.g., an attack ad, a price cut or a distribution push and then sitting back. The key to maneuver, as we can see from Boyd and from TLC loop thinking, is to surprise the competitor, find its weakness and then to pursue the advantage by committing resources when a point of weakness is observed.

One example from my own experience was in the beer industry when a major competitor had just gone through a difficult hostile takeover. The sales forces of the two merged brewers were, we believed, feeling insecure and the future portfolio of beers was unclear. The target market here was free pubs (i.e., pubs that were not tied to one or other of the brewers to buy their beer) and the goal was customer acquisition. My client therefore launched an aggressive campaign consisting of a combination of promotions, advertising and sales visits to pubs that stocked the competitor beers in order to gain trial.

By keeping strong control on the campaign, with weekly reports at local, regional and national level, my client was able to see where different approaches were working, where the weaknesses truly lay (they found that the morale problem actually sat with the salesmen of one of the companies but not the other) and which regions or competitor products were most vulnerable to attack. Each week the campaign could be adjusted to reflect these findings and to direct resources and creativity into the weaknesses. This attack period of only around 2 months resulted in a lasting gain of share. It was not clear whether the competitor, absorbed in its internal problems, even noticed that this attack was happening – the ultimate surprise!

Another example is in the car industry. Many people buy new cars and then sell them when they are around three years old. Historically, customers have tended to buy cars from the same marque (brand, such as VW, Ford or Toyota), perhaps trading up to a larger car model over time. This means a particularly interesting opportunity is a "conquest" sale – i.e., getting someone to shift over to your marque from another. Typically dealerships have not been very creative in identifying this target market, nor at over-investing in them.

But some dealers have shown much greater creativity. For example, I came across one dealership that sent its salesmen out in their hometown looking for competitor cars that were around three years old. They then left cards on the windscreens of these cars offering a test drive and attractive trade-in terms to the owners of these cars. This led to a surprising number of enquiries – and as any car dealer will tell you it is getting these initial enquiries that is the key to a conquest sale. It worked in part because the competitor dealers did not have their own agility in place – which would have been to note all cars that were coming up to three years old from their own records and proactively contact the owners with an offer.

Another example of using superior agility to defeat slower moving competitors is from our old favorite, credit cards. When Marks and Spencer (M&S) decided to upgrade its store card to a fully-fledged credit card (i.e., one that could be used anywhere) it faced the challenge of attacking major incumbents in a market where everybody had at least one card. The major player was Barclaycard, owned by the British bank Barclays. M&S's major target segment was older women who did not have their own credit card and were additional cardholders on their husbands' cards, but who did have an M&S store card.

Barclaycard had long followed an attritional set of marketing tactics, investing enormous amounts in brand advertising. M&S adopted a little known aspect of its Terms and Conditions to upgrade its customers' cards without requiring an "opt-in" choice. This meant that the target customers received a fully functional credit card whether or not they asked for it.

In addition, the card was launched with a loyalty scheme offering discounts on M&S shopping. This allowed M&S to target offers to core customers at short notice that met the need of the broader retail chain – whether it was double points on specific Fridays to boost overall sales, or extra points for products or categories where sales growth was being targeted. The advantage in agility came from the fact that Barclaycard, without the loyalty scheme, could only respond through price offers – which by regulation they could only make after a one month delay and to more customers that just those targeted by M&S. At the time Barclaycard's CRM systems were not sufficiently sophisticated to defend this attack directly, although as they began to notice the loss in share they did respond with further attritional attacks, including price offers. This aggressive move by M&S resulted in the largest credit card launch outside the United States, and the fastest growing credit card ever in Europe.

(Interestingly, the major barrier to agility in the credit card market is regulation. Most marketing activities require advance warning of planned changes in terms and conditions. As with Ryanair and its advertising, Marks and Spencer's approach resulted in a public dispute with the regulator, the Office of Fair Trading. Regulators are not set up to deal with agility, even when this is in the customer's best interests.)

M&S could not pursue the Maneuver Marketing strategy much further because it too had its own slow processes – in this case supply chain procedures that meant it could only order large quantities of long lead-time items for specific loyalty offers. Tesco with its shorter supply chain was able to do many more of these short term attacking moves through its Clubcard.

An early version of this was when opening a new store. Tesco was able to use its Clubcard information to identify Tesco shoppers that were in the catchment area of the new store, and also whether these were currently main shoppers at Tesco or elsewhere (as could be seen from the absence of certain telltale items from the shopping baskets or from the frequency of visit). Tesco was then able to send out targeted vouchers in advance of the new store opening, with time limited offers, to attract these shoppers to trial the new store. Then over the following months it was able both to adapt the store to what seemed to work and to adjust the mailings to more specifically target different segments. All the while the competitors' stores could only respond in a general way to the opening of a new store without any customized tailoring.

In some cases, supermarkets have offered to redeem points on competitor loyalty cards in order to attract their competitors' most loyal shoppers into the store. This will only really work as a Maneuver Marketing tactic, though, if the next step is a rapid attack on the competitor by examining items on the loyalty card statement and promoting offers aimed specifically at each individual. The original competitor may have no idea this is happening, and certainly no agile way of responding, while a blunt price reduction on everything to everyone would be far too expensive – an example where an incumbent cannot use Attritional Marketing to defeat a Maneuver Marketing attack.

More recently, mobile telephone operators have adopted similar approaches based on their CRM capabilities. Following the initial wave of attracting new customers to the market, the battleground has become existing mobile phone users as they come out of fixed length contract – either to acquire them for a different operator, or retain them. As CRM systems were built, it became possible to make individualized offers to customers who were thinking of defecting to a competitor. I have recently experienced a good example of this as a customer. Having switched from T-Mobile to O2 a couple of years ago, I was contacted by a salesman from T-Mobile (who have just merged in the UK with Orange), asking if I was about to consider switching suppliers. (Since they knew I had switched to O2 because it was the only provider of an iPhone at the time, and that a typical contract is 24 months, this was a smart move. They were able to start a conversation about a switch and target O2 very specifically on price and service.)

WHEN SHOULD DIFFERENT FORMS OF MARKETING BE USED?

I have now introduced four different styles of marketing – Evolutionary Marketing, Big Leap Marketing, Attritional Marketing and Maneuver Marketing.

In the previous chapter I discussed when Big Leap Marketing might be required for innovation compared to Evolutionary Marketing. The criteria I set out were designed to identify when agility was likely to be practicable to build as a capability. The three traditional ways to help companies identify what approaches to use are:

1. To adopt a **capability based lens** (i.e., if you are good at this sort of thing, do this), or
2. To adopt the lens of what **your objective** is (i.e., if you want to achieve this, do this).
3. To adopt the lens of **market position** (i.e., in this sort of a market position, do this).

My proposal is to combine the capability based lens with the objective lens.

(There is one existing attempt to define the marketing approach based on the lens of market position, which I will discuss at the end of this chapter - Ries & Trout, *Marketing Warfare* (1986). This refers to four different approaches to marketing, although they do not map easily onto the four types of marketing I have introduced. For those readers familiar with Ries & Trout's work, at the end of the chapter I will show how the two approaches interrelate.)

A framework for choosing the marketing approach

Specifically, I suggest using a combination of whether you are agile or not, and whether your strategic objective is to shape, adapt or to beat competitors (see Figure 11-2). These three strategic stances, you will recall, arise directly from the three elements of my definition of marketing.

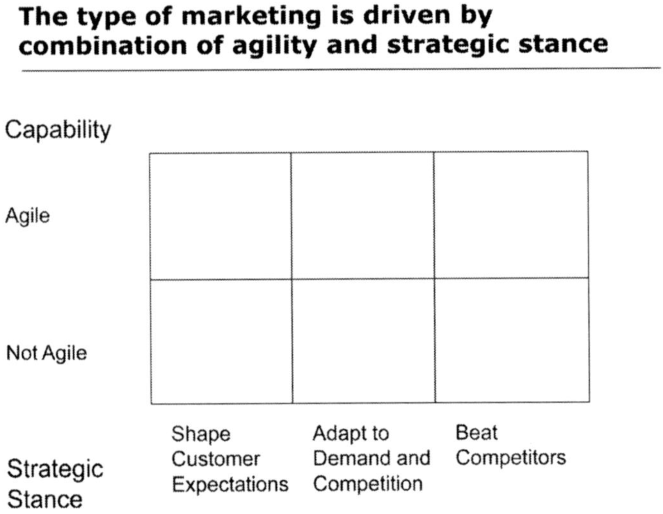

The type of marketing is driven by combination of agility and strategic stance

Figure 11-2

We saw earlier that Evolutionary Marketing is an attractive approach when you are agile and attempting either to shape customer expectations or to adapt to demand and competition. (Figure 11-3)

Evolutionary marketing is for agile businesses seeking to shape or adapt to customer demand

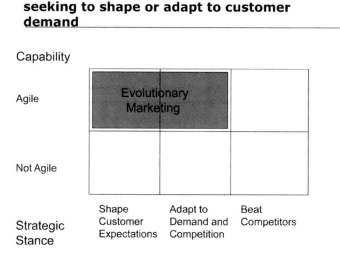

Figure 11-3

We saw in the last Chapter that a Big Leap approach to innovation is appropriate either when you are not agile, or if the challenge of shaping customer expectation is too great even for rapid TLC loops. Therefore the Big Leap overlaps the Evolutionary Marketing on this matrix (Figure 11-4).

Big Leaps are both a way of adapting when not agile and of shaping whatever the agility

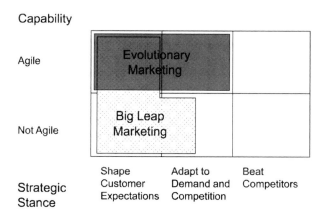

Figure 11-4

Finally, we saw that Maneuver Marketing is a way to beat competitors when you have the necessary agility, while Attritional Marketing is a way of beating competitors when you are not agile (Figure 11-5).

Maneuver and attritional marketing focus more on competitors than on customers

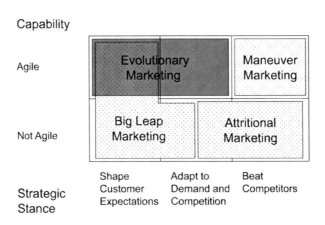

Figure 11-5

This then completes the matrix.

Ries & Trout: Marketing Warfare

In 1986, Al Ries and Jack Trout wrote a book called "Marketing Warfare," declaring "marketing is war where the enemy is the competition and the customer is the ground to be won." This perspective of marketing is obviously very close to the one underlying Maneuver Marketing. They argue that there are four ways to fight a marketing war: Defensive, Offensive, Flanking and Guerrilla. How do their four ways relate to the concept of Maneuver Marketing?

The answer is that they are different lenses on the same problem. Ries & Trout's four ways related primarily to the market position of the players. Their strategic square (Figure 11-6) is based on the size of the company and hence their relative resources.

RIES & TROUT'S STRATEGIC SQUARE

Defensive For Market Leaders	Offensive For No. 2 Companies
Flanking For Smaller Companies	Guerrilla For local or regional companies

Figure 11-6

"Reproduced with permission of The McGraw-Hill Companies from Ries & Trout (1986) Marketing Warfare."

In this it takes a similar approach to the BCG portfolio matrix,[12] which also considers strategy for individual business units as being related to their market position. On the other hand, the contrast between Attrition and Maneuver Marketing is a resource or capability based view. Obviously a company that lacked agility could not adopt Maneuver Marketing as a strategy whatever their market position.

However, there are areas where the two lenses provide similar perspectives. Broadly speaking, Ries & Trout argue that market leaders should play defensively by creating innovations themselves before competitors do and blocking strong competitive moves. They can afford to do this because they have greater resources and thus can win what is broadly speaking a war of attrition. However, I am arguing that if, in addition, the market leader can have fast TLC loops their "defensive warfare" need not be warfare at all – they can pursue Evolutionary Marketing and be not only strong but also clever. By always being one step ahead of competition they will not be vulnerable to attack but will win by always serving customers better.

Number 2 companies on the other hand cannot pursue attrition, so they MUST be agile to win. Ries & Trout argue that they need to attack weaknesses in the market leader and put as much force into a narrow area of attack as possible. This is the essence of Maneuver Marketing based on agility: Test and Learn to find an offer that it stronger than the competition and then Commit to focus all your resources at the weak point.

The third approach discussed by Ries & Trout is Flanking. In both the military and in the view of Ries & Trout these are attempts to find an uncontested area, almost certainly including tactical surprise. These moves may be achieved through Evolutionary Marketing by finding a part of the fitness landscape where existing competitors are weak, but it may require a Big Leap into an uncontested area rather than continuous improvement. This possibility was the subject of Chapter 10.

Finally, what Ries & Trout call Guerrilla warfare is for the vast majority of companies that are too small to dominate an entire market, but instead find a niche to defend – while being willing to give it up if a larger competitor launches an overwhelming attack. These players probably have just the single option if they are to survive: being agile. The difference between them and overall market leaders is that they are just trying to be the fittest in a small part of the market landscape. So long as they adopt Evolutionary Marketing in that area, they should be able to maintain fitness at a "local optimum" for a long time. It does not matter to them that there may be fitter parts of the overall landscape – in mathematical terms a "global optimum." However for the market leader it is a serious problem if it finds itself at a local optimum since it means there is an opportunity for someone else to occupy the fittest global position. In that case the market leader may have been outflanked and need itself to adopt a Big Leap, as discussed in the last chapter.

Maneuver Marketing is a simple idea based on fast TLC loops. Yet there seem to be surprisingly few examples of it being used in practice. While the strategic marketing approach that attacks competitors without benefiting customers may be anti-cultural for many companies, the more customer friendly approach of Virgin Atlantic has great potential. Even more so, the potential for tactical Maneuver Marketing campaigns is very high. With new technologies, especially CRM, the opportunity to develop and control Maneuver Marketing campaigns is greater than ever before. Yet this does not seem to be happening to any great extent, possibly in part because the concepts are not yet understood by most marketers, but even more so because businesses are insufficiently agile. The challenge therefore is to develop the necessary agility, which is the topic of Part 5 of this book.

NOTES

1   Von Clausewitz, C. (1827). *On War.* 1997. Ware, Herts.: Wordsworth Editions.

2   Sun Tzu. *The Art of War.* 2001. Boston: Shambhala.

3   Ries, A. & Trout, J. (1986). *Marketing Warfare* (20th Anniversary ed.). 2006. New York: McGraw-Hill.

4   Stalk, G. Jr. & Hout, T. M. (1990). *Competing Against Time.* New York: Free Press.

5   Peters, T. (1987). *Thriving on Chaos.* New York: Alfred A. Knopf.

6   Richards, C. (2004). *Certain to Win.* Atlanta: Xlibris. This book examines how the philosophy and approaches can be applied to business broadly and also explains how Toyota's production system is based on the same concept of agility.

7   Ibid. p. 65.

8   Bungay, S. (2000). *The Most Dangerous Enemy.* London: Aurum Press.

9   Handley, L. (2010, July 1). Mind the Gap. *Marketing Week.*

10   OFT investigation halts Ryanair ad complaints, By Gemma Charles, marketingmagazine.co.uk, 27 May 2009

11   Citizen Strategist, http://www.citizenstrategist.com/, Mike Smock.

12   Anon. (1970). *The Product Portfolio.* Boston: Boston Consulting Group.

PART 5

DESIGNING THE AGILE MARKETING ORGANIZATION

Back in Chapter 1, I stated that I initially believed that the challenge in becoming customer-centric was largely organizational. This book was going to be all about meeting that challenge. However, once I discovered the importance of agility, in the form of fast-loop marketing, in meeting the three key criteria of fitness, speed and efficiency, the focus of the book became this new approach to marketing. But now the time has come to address the organizational question. How should businesses organize to deliver Agile Marketing?

My answer has three elements (Figure 12-1):

- First, the business needs an organization structure that fits its strategy and its competitive landscape. For large, complex businesses this should be what is known as a hybrid matrix structure.
- Second, the business needs a rapid response culture that combines customer focus with entrepreneurial initiative to encourage and support fast-loop marketing.
- Third, the business needs to combine its processes, people, tools and metrics into a Commercial Operating System that will reliably enable rapid response to changes in the market.

Organizing for Agile Marketing

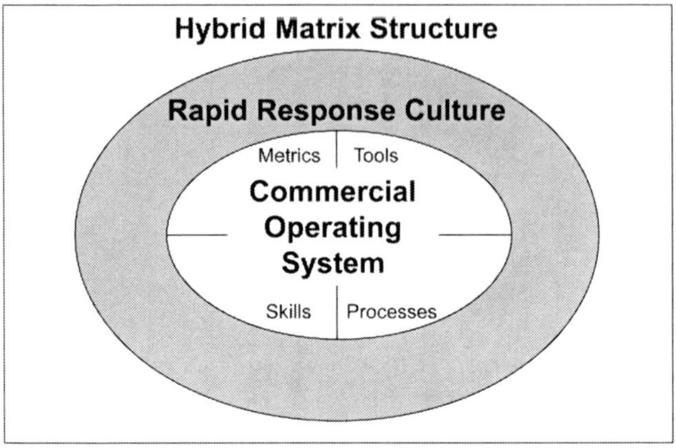

Figure 12-1

The importance of structure and of culture should come as no surprise. You are most likely unfamiliar, however, with the concept of a Commercial Operating System (COS). This is a blueprint for how the company does sales and marketing in the two or three areas (such as pricing, brand, segment, channel, or key-account management) that are most closely linked to a company's strategic Priorities.[1] It is best thought of as the "Company Way" of marketing and sales.

I use the term "Commercial" rather than "Marketing" here to emphasize that this is a system that goes beyond the functional boundaries of marketing or even sales. One of the prime challenges of being customer-centric in Agile Marketing is to integrate the activities of all the executional functions behind the marketing experiments and rollouts. The entire business's executional capabilities need to support an agile approach to marketing. I will show that by paying close attention to the COS a manager can shape the way the organization will respond to the market.

In the next three chapters I will look in turn at structure, culture and the Commercial Operating System. My belief is that the non-structural elements of the fast-loop marketing organization are the trickiest to manage, since this is where the challenges of fast-loop marketing differ most radically from the more usual approaches to designing customer-centric organizations.

NOTES

1   Webb, A. (Ed.). (2006). *Profiting from Proliferation*, New York: McKinsey & Company.

CHAPTER 12

STRUCTURE

Structure is the most obvious aspect of organization design, and one that has been extensively studied as a means of enabling more customer-centric organizations. In this chapter I will recap much of the earlier work, explaining where some adjustments may be needed to facilitate Agile Marketing. I have provided some specific references if you wish to delve more deeply into this topic.

PREVIOUS WORK ON ORGANIZATION

Let me first summarize briefly two of the best books on customer-centric organization - by George Day and Jay Galbraith.

George Day: The Market Driven Organization

George Day, a Professor at the Wharton School of the University of Pennsylvania, has written about marketing for many years and wrote "The Market Driven Organization" in response to the failure of many organizations to execute against the exhortation to stay close to the customer and ahead of the competition.[1]

Day argues that one of the prime objectives of becoming more market-driven is to build relevant organizational capabilities. He proposes three required capabilities: market sensing, creating customer relationships, and strategic thinking.

By market sensing, Day means a combination of gathering information about the market, making sense of that information based on the company's mental models, and storing this knowledge in an information base that acts as organizational memory and can be accessed throughout the organization. This capability captures many of the same elements

I identified earlier in this book: a combination of market research, knowing your market landscape and immersion in the customer experience. The main difference between Day's thesis and mine arises from my search for speed through intuition more than through pursuing analysis.

Day's focus on customer relationships follows the management theory that retaining customers is a uniquely profitable strategic lever. While I agree in principle, more recent research has suggested that the early work on customer loyalty overstated its benefits.[2] In some marketplaces loyalty may be critical, but not in all. So rather than a focus on relationship building, I prefer a broader range of capabilities, more tailored to an individual business environment.

Finally, Day's view of the capability for thinking strategically encompasses two underlying factors: depth of market understanding and planning processes that adapt to the real environment. He describes an approach to planning that merges top down guidance and resource allocation with bottom up market knowledge. In this last he has anticipated Bungay's approach to planning in Big Leap Marketing. However there is far less emphasis on experimentation, although Day does mention it (e.g., p. 91 and p. 241).

Day focuses on how to build these capabilities, but also discusses how best to align the organization to the market. He identifies a hybrid organization structure that combines the best elements of vertical functional forms with horizontal process organizations as the likely way forward. However, he notes that structure is only part of the organizational solution. The other elements he considers to be part of market orientation are the capabilities discussed above, the organizational culture, a shared knowledge base for collecting and disseminating market insights, and a "*configuration* that enables the entire organization continually to anticipate and respond to changing customer requirements and market conditions." (p. 7) This configuration includes not only the organization design, but also the executional capabilities for delivering customer value and all the supporting systems, controls, measures and human resource policies.

Jay Galbraith: Designing the Customer-Centric Organization

Jay Galbraith is an expert on organization design who was struck by how hard most companies found it to become customer-centric. His book (2005)[3] was based on 14 case studies, conducted in collaboration with a McKinsey research team.

Galbraith's work is centered on the trend in business-to-business marketing towards solutions. Like Day he recognizes the need to tailor the organization design to the strategy of the business. He stresses, however, that most companies talk about a complexity of solutions marketing whose scale and scope require far greater integration between functions and business units than their organization is able to deliver. Consequently, his recommended approach for these more complex strategies is itself very complex. However he too arrives at some form of hybrid organization, combining, in his words, a "customer-centric front end with a product-centric back end." (p. 87)

His work is full of detailed case studies and is an excellent source to understand the challenges and pitfalls of transforming from a product-centered approach to a solutions-centered approach. Like Day, he argues that structure is just one of the elements of a successful organization, adding to it alignment between the structure and four other elements – the strategy, the processes, the reward systems and the people (human resource) policies.

HOW AGILE MARKETING AFFECTS THE ORGANIZATIONAL SOLUTION

It is clear that previous work on customer centricity is agreed that one of the prime objectives of becoming more market-driven is to build relevant organizational capabilities. This is supported by my own work. Each of the client companies I surveyed about their efforts to be more customer oriented identified a challenge in filling the capability gaps to deliver the strategic and organizational vision: e.g., "At the moment we are investing in a customer segmentation project and a new customer service frontline system to help tailor our customer interactions, but the managers have no idea how to link the two or start testing new customer treatments" (Marketing Director of global utilities retailer).

At McKinsey, we were early in studying this problem. In 1994 I wrote an article introducing the hybrid organization with two of my partners,[4] which was then extended by other colleagues.[5] As we gained more practical expertise in helping companies transform, it became clear that the hybrid structural solutions that are broadly common to our work, to Day and to Galbraith, were adequate for the task, but that the non-structural elements were more challenging to implement. This led to our own development of the supporting elements to strategy and structure, that we termed the Commercial Operating System.[6]

An important feature of successful marketing is the need for integration: internal integration across functions and processes, and external integration with partners across the supply chain. In contrast to traditional consumer goods companies where the marketing department has control over the offer, in other industries this is not the case. In service businesses such as retailing, and in solutions businesses, the marketing isn't in control of all aspects of the offer, so there is a real need to get cross-departmental coordination to make trade-offs and experiments in the offer.

For example, you can market a department store by: investing more in store design or spending more on getting prime sites (traditionally the responsibility of the property department), by doing more classical advertising (traditionally the responsibility of the marketing department), by spending more on direct marketing via the credit card (often the responsibility of the finance director), by adding more sales personnel to get better service (responsibility of store management), or by cutting price on garments (responsibility of buyers). The organizational solution has to be able to cope with all these trade-offs and all this coordination. This is the main reason why the supporting elements are introduced: to strengthen the basic organizational structure.

However, even though previous work provides a consensus, the struggle to become customer-centric is, in practice, largely unsolved. I believe that this is because none of the earlier work takes account of the challenges of Evolutionary and Maneuver Marketing, as I have outlined them in this book. I therefore believe that although previous work accurately documents how companies attempt to organize to deliver traditional marketing (typically a combination of Attritional and Big Leap Marketing), it inevitably leads to eventual disappointment when the landscape changes too rapidly for these forms of marketing.

Trying to plan your way to rapid adaptation is doomed to failure. Businesses following only this path therefore had limited success, providing ample fodder for those who wanted to resist the market oriented approach. This in turn meant at best a muddled view at all levels of the organization of the benefits of market orientation. Against this context, it is unsurprising that successes were few and far between.

The organization needs to be designed to execute both Evolutionary and Maneuver Marketing. Nevertheless, as I discussed in the previous chapter, sometimes Big Leap Marketing or Attritional marketing is appropriate, so the organization needs to be able to work in this way, too.

THE HYBRID MATRIX

My goal, then, is to combine the best of the earlier work with the additional need that I have identified for agility. Businesses trying to implement Agile Marketing must combine the lessons that have been learned in becoming more market-oriented in the traditional approaches with those learned by organizations trying to be more agile.

Many organizations find that their existing organization structure interferes with their market orientation. Experience shows in particular that traditional product-focused organizations struggle to deliver customer-focused strategies. In a survey we conducted at McKinsey, over half the marketing capability building projects we examined included an organizational restructuring.

The most common problem they faced was the need to clarify individual responsibilities and to ensure better coordination between functions responsible for understanding and delivering to customers.

- The main structural challenge the businesses faced was to create one coordinated approach to the customer: "The brand, telesales and web marketing managers are all pursuing their own individual targets and plans and we have even heard of customers playing them off against each other" (Sales Director of European retail asset manager).
- There was also frequently a challenge to ensure that all functions were focused on delivering the same strategic goals: "We could not roll out the (successful) cross-selling pilots because the individual product areas are focused on their own annual P&L and so cannot agree how to apportion revenues and the incremental costs" (Sales Director of UK insurer).

This has led most businesses to explore alternative dimensions around which to organize. Typically they adopt hybrid matrix structures.

As George Day points out (1999, pp. 186-208),[7] any attempt to improve alignment around the customer requires balancing several contending forces, all of which are familiar in organization design more generally. These include:

Maintaining flexibility through small units	versus	Achieving economies of scale
Aligning with market and geographies	versus	Leveraging distinctive capabilities
Being innovative	versus	Being reliable
Building specialist expertise	versus	Industrializing cross-functional processes
Facilitating coordination and information sharing	versus	Eliminating overhead and unproductive activities

Anyone with hands-on experience of organization design will recognize these trade-offs. Early responses to the dilemma sought new dimensions around which to organize. These included Customer segments, Industry, Brand, Geography, Channel, and Functions in addition to product. Typically all this achieved was to improve performance on the new organizational dimension at the cost of performance in the others. Then the idea of a matrix took hold, with a secondary organizational dimension put in place to attempt to have your cake and eat it. For example a global product/geography matrix would allow marketers to focus on their own product areas, but sales forces in each country could combine their selling efforts to common customers.[8] Over time these matrices have become increasingly complicated to work in and have slowed down decision processes, which is especially worrying for fast-loop marketing.

For example, in one global financial services company, the new Country Manager for the UK found herself able to take very few decisions without extensive consultations. She found herself in Sydney for the entire first week of her appointment discussing new product ideas. On returning to London, she discovered that the parent company had decided not to respond to a new regulation in the UK because the head office strategists, who did not know the UK market, had decided it did not make sense. Once this had been sorted out (taking a couple of months) she then had to negotiate with the IT department in the US to free some resources to enable the change (a change that was compulsory, remember). Then the Global Marketing Group needed to be involved. Separately, her peers on the European Management Board needed to be persuaded that the additional budget required to implement this change should be released. Only then could she focus on operational matters, at which point some necessary changes to the local call center needed to be discussed with the Global Call Operations division. All this was for an entirely obvious change that the competitors had each put in place months previously.

In the 1990's the fashion for process reengineering, combined with dissatisfaction with matrix organizations led to a theory that new "horizontal" organization designs should be very flat and non-hierarchical, based around core processes. However very few businesses attempted to move to a pure horizontal organization, so instead various hybrid forms were developed. These hybrid forms combine horizontal business processes managed by teams with specialist functions, together with other integrating mechanisms. More recently some companies have tried to use IT to deepen and broaden the availability of information around the organization as a way to avoid some of the complexity that used to be caused by the need for physical collocation.

From the numerous experiments that have been tried, I would pinpoint two key components of a successful marketing organization:

1. **Integrators.** There needs to be someone integrating strategy and operations around the dimensions of the business with the greatest opportunity to create value. They may be traditional BU heads, or process team leaders, but they need to be accountable for developing customer-focused value propositions and end-to-end delivery. They will be marketers with broad skills who have a holistic picture of the market environment to develop the necessary Situation Awareness. They should lead the TLC loop process for Agile Marketing and the ADAM process for Big Leap Marketing. They will need to be developed through an apprenticeship system (see the Commercial Operating System in the next chapter) and will be the natural mentors for future integrators.

2. **Specialists.** The new tools and frameworks will require people who have specialized functional skills. They are likely to have different competences from the integrators, being passionate about developing deep technical marketing skills, for example in market research, advertising, pricing or data analysis. They work best in centers of excellence, where they can learn from each other and follow a specialized career structure. The organization needs to ensure that they can easily be assigned to process teams when needed.

The organization structure that results from this, in generalized form, looks as in Figure 12-2. There are several teams, seen on the right of the diagram, with responsibility for core processes, each led by an integrator, and several specialist groupings, providing centers of excellence in skills such as advertising, digital media and market research. For greater details of these types of structure I refer you to the books by Day and Galbraith, as well as the published work from McKinsey.

Matrix Marketing Organization

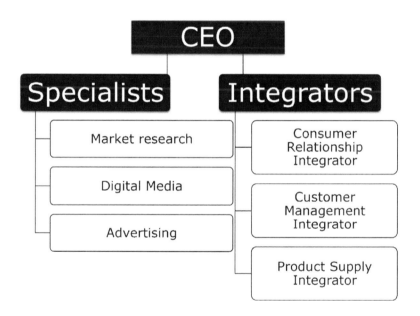

Figure 12-2

The main difference between my proposals for marketing and the ingoing assumptions from previous work is that I see an imperative for rapid experimentation. So my organizational recommendations reflect that imperative. However, I believe that this combination of specialists and integrators is vital both for traditional plan-based marketing and for Agile Marketing. This is because Agile Marketing depends on a marketer close to the front-line taking entrepreneurial initiative. This marketer will be part of an integrative team, able to pull expertise from specialists as needed. The key organizational difference is likely to be not in structure, but in the culture. Often managers assume that the integrative teams should be run in a command and control approach – the integrator says what should be done, and the junior team members do it. For Agile Marketing, however, the more junior members can only ensure sufficient speed around the loop by taking the initiative, based on their own Situation Awareness, and running new experiments as well as winnowing out failed ones.

Because very few organizations are yet attempting Agile Marketing, I cannot point clearly to how they would differ from more traditional customer-centric organizations. However my belief is that this added desire for front-line entrepreneurs will affect the relative importance placed on central functional teams. For example, the stores operations function of a retail organization has traditionally assumed that local store managers do what they are told by either Head Office or the Regional Manager, because store managers have lower strategic skills. Since Agile Marketing emphasizes Situation Awareness and rapid execution over strategic skills, this logic (if ever true) is not valid. So the organization boxes may look the same, but the detailed responsibilities and interactions will be different.

In addition, every organization structure leaves activities and decisions that can fall between the gaps. In order to catch these gaps, coordinating mechanisms are needed to complement the structure. Examples of coordinating mechanisms are lead markets (perhaps to conduct more experiments), communities of interest (some consumer companies have special interest groups focusing on the grey market, for example), or IT tools such as internal social networks.

For this reason, when designing organization structures I recommend augmenting the usual pictures of boxes and outline responsibilities with job descriptions that include who each jobholder is most likely to interact with, what information or tools he will need to do his job, and how much time is likely to be spent on different areas of the job.[9]

⟐

In this chapter we have seen that Agile Marketing in a large business will almost inevitably demand a revised organization structure. It should be a hybrid matrix, tailored to the target segments, based around integrators who are accountable for developing customer-focused value propositions and end-to-end delivery, and marketing specialists who work in centers of excellence and are assigned to process teams as needed. The structure will need to be complemented by coordinating mechanisms to fill the gaps between the structural boxes and accountabilities. The culture and the Commercial Operating System must then both be developed to support this structure.

NOTES

1   Day, G. S. (1999). *The Market Driven Organization*. New York: Free Press.

2   Palmer, A., (Ed.) (2003). *Refreshing the challenge of relationship marketing: proceedings of the 11th International Colloquium in Relationship Marketing.*, Cheltenham: University of Gloucestershire.

3   Galbraith, J. R. (2005). *Designing the Customer-Centric Organization*. San Francisco: Jossey-Bass.

4   George, M., Freeling, A. & Court, D. (1994). Reinventing the Marketing Organization. *McKinsey Quarterly 1994* (4), 43-62.

5   Aufreiter, N., George, M. & Lempres, L. (1996). Developing a Distinctive Consumer Marketing Organization. *Journal of Market-Focused Management 1996*, 3, 199-208.

6   See, e.g., Knudsen, T.R., Moret, C. & Van Metre, E. S. (2006). The power of a Commercial Operating System. In Webb, (Ed.) *Profiting from Proliferation* pp. 61-71. (This definition includes structure within the Commercial Operating System; I have pulled it out since it is a specific lever often pulled prior to a concerted attempt to build a new COS.)

7   Day, G. S. (1999). *The Market Driven Organization.*

8   Riesenbeck, H. & Freeling, A. (1991). Global Brands. *McKinsey Quarterly 1991*, 4, pp. 3-18.

9   These job descriptions, whilst very useful, are not intended to dictate exactly how the jobholder should work in the role. Instead, they are best seen as an aid to closing the alignment gap for the flexible organization. They communicate the intent of the organization that has been designed, but the details will need to be adapted to changing situations.

CHAPTER 13

CULTURE

I cannot claim to be the first to propose that culture is key to a successful organizational shift. Indeed all the previous research into market orientation points to the importance of a culture that values customers and meeting their needs. When asked, executives who are seeking to develop improved market orientation identify the challenge of sustainably changing mind-sets and behaviors: "Our biggest challenge in delivering this new design is going to be how we make sure that the business unit managers don't just revert to doing things the way that they have always done them" (HR Director of North American utilities retailer).

Culture has similarly been found to be fundamental to executing fast-loops (although in his military work John Boyd used the term "organization climate" to describe culture). In this chapter I shall pull together the various strands regarding culture in the literature on market orientation, in my research on commercial transformation, and from John Boyd regarding rapid OODA loops.

George Day argues that market-driven behavior is embedded in the shared values, norms and beliefs that give members of an organization meaning and provide them with rules for behaving. He contrasts them with the values of more self-centered organizations (1999, p. 45),[1] for example:

- All decisions start with the customer, not with the company
- Living with customers to learn about them, not viewing all customer interactions as an opportunity to sell
- Valuing information about customers, including those who have defected, and disseminating it, not focusing only on new prospects and hoarding information to enhance power.

- Using research to improve decisions, not merely to satisfy curiosity or to sell a decision
- Being paranoid about competitors rather than copying them or arrogantly ignoring them
- Learning from mistakes versus punishing risk takers.

He also stresses that the tone of the organization is set at the top and that the culture must be continuously nurtured, since if actions are taken that are against customer interests this is very rapidly observed by employees, partners and customers. At times of cost cutting, this risk is especially salient.

The good news is that these findings about culture are consistent with the four characteristics of the organizational climate that Boyd identified would ensure faster OODA loops, which are themselves consistent with the cultural principles underlying the Toyota Production system and other fast-loop systems. He arrived at these principles by analyzing how the German army executed the Blitzkrieg, which was the greatest modern example of successful rapid OODA loops. In the remainder of this chapter, therefore, I will go through Boyd's principles[2] and suggest how they can support TLC marketing (Figure 13-1).

Boyd's first principle is to **exploit intuitive knowledge, or "feel"**. I have already argued that this is critical to rapid OODA loops. It enables people to observe more than is obvious and to be able to orient rapidly and thus maintain speed in the OODA loop. It requires competence not only in the theoretical aspects of marketing, but more importantly in the environment in which they are placing marketing offers to compete. As I have argued repeatedly, this can only be gained by experience and on the job training. It is why I doubt that companies or individuals with experience in different environments can automatically be successful in the new environment (e.g., bringing experts in shampoos into food, or even into banking).

Culture: Speed up TLC loops with Boyd's "elements of the Blitzkrieg"

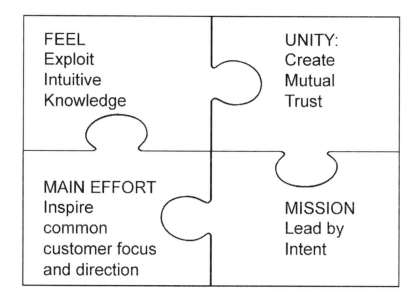

FEEL
Exploit
Intuitive
Knowledge

UNITY:
Create
Mutual
Trust

MAIN EFFORT
Inspire
common
customer focus
and direction

MISSION
Lead by
Intent

Figure 13-1

Boyd's second principle is to **create mutual trust, or "unity"**. In a discussion of how Boyd's principles can be applied to business, Chet Richards (2005, p. 101)[3] argues that the key element of organization unity is mutual trust, which is what converts a mob into a team. If the individual members of a team have the intuitive knowledge, unity ensures that each individual's effort is harmonized with the group goal – its main effort. This means that on the one hand individuals know what they need to achieve, and on the other hand that their colleagues trust them to act in ways that will achieve it. This mutual trust speeds up the OODA loops more than anything else, since checks and balances do not need to be put in place in case people do the wrong thing. Similarly, it eases integration between marketing and other functions to improve executional efficiency, which again speeds up OODA loops.

The most important insight into mutual trust from both military and business applications is that trust must be earned. It can't be taught in classrooms or exhorted by leaders: it can only be forged in the heat of battle or competition. Only when things have been difficult and a team's individuals have jointly pulled through does the team really gain the requisite level of trust. Conversely, top managers can kill trust in them very quickly by demonstrating a lack of trust in their people. Managers often do this without realizing it by seeking to control what their staff members do, as opposed to directing what they should achieve. Equally, lapses in ethics or pay deals that are seen as egregious all contribute to a lack of trust. In my experience, most management teams do not really act as if they truly believe that trust is important (although they never admit it). But to an outsider, and even more to a subordinate, where there is a lack of trust the problem is immediately obvious.

The third principle Boyd identifies is to **inspire common customer focus and direction** – the **"main effort"**. It helps align everyone by answering the question "what is to be done?" Our research at McKinsey identified that a critical element of culture is a top team leading an entire organization that is aligned around a simple yet aspirational customer-facing theme. The aspiration might be expressed as a financial goal, or as a broader aspiration to excellence, such as Steve Jobs' challenge to Apple to make "insanely great" products. In all cases it provided a clear focus for every individual's effort and was continually reinforced in the light of customer and competitor reactions.

My more recent research reinforces this finding, together with the importance of the culture encouraging people to identify imaginative solutions to problems and to bring new ideas to life. This may seem obvious or even trite, but in fact it is surprisingly hard to maintain focus as the situation changes, so top management will need continually to reinforce the focus. It demands clarity on who is being targeted: the customer segments upon which the business will focus (which in turn helps everyone be clear what their individual role is). Note though, that in both warfare and business, the main effort can evolve over time, as the opponent or customer changes, usually unpredictably. So the initial customer segment focus can still change in light of market reality.

Boyd's fourth principle is to **lead by intent – "mission"**, rather than leading by orders. As I have already discussed, my colleague at Ashridge, Stephen Bungay, has written about applying leadership by intent to planning. To quote from his work:

"The two core demands are to establish a high level of alignment by being very clear about 'what' and 'why', and to grant a high measure of decision-making authority to relatively low levels of the organization who are dealing with the question of 'how'. Rather than following detailed orders, an officer's responsibility is to understand his commander's *intention* and to take whatever action he deems necessary to fulfill it. If the situation changes – as it is expected to – the guide to decision-making is the original intent.

"It can be understood as a form of what we would today call 'empowerment'. It involves creating space for decision-making by giving power to those who need it, and not allowing it to be withheld by those who do not. Decision levels should be set as low as possible. This also reduces the need for all but essential information to be passed up and down the chain of command, ensuring that decisions are taken by the competent individual with the most up-to-date information. The combination of aligning everyone about 'what' and 'why' and pushing down decision-making results in an organization that can adapt rapidly in the face of uncertainty, whilst retaining cohesion."[4]

A business whose culture follows these four principles is very well placed to adopt the principles of Agile Marketing. I personally believe this is the most important, but also trickiest part of building the fast-loop marketing capability, because if you have the culture your people will make every effort to achieve the main effort, even if held back by out of date organizational structures and dysfunctional Commercial Operating Systems. But equally without a supportive structure and a working Commercial Operating System, morale will inevitably dip, and questions about top management will, quite rightly, be asked. So the culture both enables, but also depends on, the other two organizational elements.

In this chapter I have shown that the culture of an Agile Marketing organization must combine the four elements that John Boyd identified for fast OODA loops: intuitive knowledge, mutual trust, a common focus and leadership by intent.

NOTES

1   Day, G. S. (1999). *The Market Driven Organization.* New York: Free Press.

2   An excellent exploration of what Boyd's concepts mean to business can be found in Richards, C. (2004). *Certain to Win.* Atlanta: Xlibris.

3   Ibid., p. 101

4   Bungay, S., Roblin, D. & Slavin, D. (2006). Taking Command. *Pharmaceutical Executive Europe,* Nov/Dec 2006, p. 40.

CHAPTER 14

THE COMMERCIAL OPERATING SYSTEM

The combination of processes, skills, tools and metrics, when properly aligned with each other and with the business strategy, constitute a distinctive Commercial Operating System (COS). This describes a blueprint for consistent marketing and sales in the key processes that are most closely linked to a company's strategic priorities (Figure 14-1).

Some of the best customer focused businesses have described their Commercial Operating Systems as a Company Way of Marketing. For example Diageo, the global drinks company has the Diageo Way of Brand Building (DWBB, pronounced Dweeb). My own research into businesses in a wide variety of industries that were seeking to transform their marketing and sales shows that they also started by describing their desired company way of marketing.

In fact, all companies have the elements of a Commercial Operating System - but very rarely do they talk about it or analyze it explicitly. This is in contrast to other functions such as production or supply chain where people will often be clear about their production operating system or their supply chain operating system. This may in part be due to the "intrinsic" nature of the knowledge in marketing and sales. Some people would argue that it couldn't be captured in processes or systematized. However, the success of a few companies such as Diageo, P&G and Capital One show that the commercial activities can in fact be described as an operating system, just as these other functional areas have been, and to great effect.

A flexible market-oriented Commercial Operating System

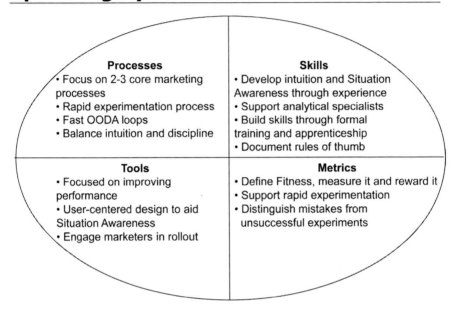

Processes
- Focus on 2-3 core marketing processes
- Rapid experimentation process
- Fast OODA loops
- Balance intuition and discipline

Skills
- Develop intuition and Situation Awareness through experience
- Support analytical specialists
- Build skills through formal training and apprenticeship
- Document rules of thumb

Tools
- Focused on improving performance
- User-centered design to aid Situation Awareness
- Engage marketers in rollout

Metrics
- Define Fitness, measure it and reward it
- Support rapid experimentation
- Distinguish mistakes from unsuccessful experiments

Figure 14-1

Unfortunately, experience shows that most commercial organizations struggle to sustain their Commercial Operating Systems. They do not pay much attention to ensuring that their processes are consistent through the organization and over time; the skill requirements for people in important roles often do not match these processes; frameworks and tools are not used consistently across the business, with much reinvention of the wheel; while the metrics and the performance management systems fail to reinforce the processes and talent management.

The result of failing to treat these elements as interlinked parts of a coherent whole can lead to disjointed efforts to apply standard tools without clarifying who will use the information, or redesigning processes without adjusting the metrics that describe success and building the talent necessary to implement them. It renders the challenge of integrating internally and externally a largely hit and miss affair.

A business needs a coherent COS whether it is trying to be an Agile Marketer or a traditional marketer. However, as I suggested earlier, a successful Commercial Operating System for Agile Marketing is likely to differ in important ways from that for Big Leaps.

This explains why some of the recommendations from consulting firms fail to "stick" in their clients. They tend to borrow from the broader experience of process reengineering and be centered on detailed prescriptions for how the marketing processes should be redesigned. They frequently introduce highly analytical tools and frameworks to execute the ADAM process, which demands extensive training for marketers who often lack the necessary quantitative skills. They also impose new, often complicated metrics aimed at ensuring that the processes were well controlled. In short, they are developed for well-planned, rigorous marketing. The resulting COS therefore does not facilitate Evolutionary Marketing, with its emphasis on rapid experimentation by seasoned, intuitive marketers.

Initially these transformational efforts are successful. External consultants, who are comfortable with this analytical approach, but who lack an intuitive insight into the marketplace, could work directly with the marketers and jointly they would make substantial improvements. However, over time, once the consultants have left, these rigorous plans fail to adapt sufficiently to the changing market landscape, proving in practice to be slow and cumbersome.

With the benefit of hindsight, far from becoming more responsive, after the consulting intervention these businesses often suffered from analysis paralysis. In addition, over 2-3 years the marketers that had been most intensively involved and trained in the new processes left and were replaced and the original less systematic approaches reappeared around the business.

The challenge, therefore, is to develop a Commercial Operating System that supports speed, fitness and efficiency, as outlined earlier, while also providing the basis for a rigorous ADAM process when required. There are, unfortunately, few organizations that have fully solved this problem, and those that have do not tend to open themselves up to detailed inspection. So in this section, I will outline some of the key features of a more agile Commercial Operating System that supports good Situation Awareness, based on the evidence I have been able to uncover so far. I shall look at the four elements of a COS separately, although always remembering that the critical need is to ensure that these elements are mutually consistent and supportive. For each one I shall look first at the requirements for fast TLC loops and then make some observations on how to provide the space for ADAM.

PROCESSES – RAPID OODA LOOPS TO SUPPORT EXPERIMENTATION

A Commercial Operating System is based upon consistent processes. These are the sequences of activities through which the relevant people interact and communicate to implement high-quality marketing and sales actions. They enable integration across different parts of a business, and by repeating the same process at different times managers can learn what works and improve.

A common problem is businesses lacking any systematic approach to managing their marketing processes. Instead, different approaches to the same marketing activity (e.g., pricing, advertising, research) are followed around the company. This both slows things down and is wasteful. The best traditional marketers such as P&G have always been distinctive for the rigor of their marketing processes. Companies that have had some success in building their market orientation have rolled out standardized processes, as Diageo did with the DWBB.

Process redesign has been one of the fads of the past couple of decades, but it has enjoyed very mixed success in practice, not least because of the scale of change that it precipitates. Sometimes it seems like every single activity of a company is being redesigned. Fortunately, as McKinsey has pointed out (2006, pp. 63 – 64),[1] it is not necessary to upend every commercial process to improve customer orientation. Instead the focus should be on the two or three key commercial processes that are central to the specific business's performance. These vary from company to company. In a drinks company I worked with, the critical processes were marketing spend effectiveness, key account management and sales force management. On the other hand, for a B2B information provider the critical processes were product development, partnering, and pricing.

My research into companies that have tried to improve customer orientation shows that these processes need to embed rapid responsiveness to changes in the market environment. For example: "Our price-setting process is built around a monthly review of our competitors' published prices…there is no formal process for collecting customer feedback on price perceptions or volume discounts" (Product Manager of European corporate bank).

In Chapter 7, I argued that this rapid responsiveness depends on smart experimentation to enable businesses to create a far greater degree of variation than previously, at lower cost. Smart experimentation needs to be embedded in the core processes within the Commercial Operating System.

Many marketing books and articles address the question of how to redesign marketing processes, but they all work on the assumption that the process should follow a deliberate, ADAM approach. Rather than repeat that work, I will focus on the challenge of ensuring that the overall processes are adapted for fast OODA loops.

- **Observation** requires an excellent flow of information from the front-line to marketing leaders. In many businesses marketing is very weak on any form of measurement, so fixing this problem has become a core plank of more traditional approaches to developing market orientation. However, gathering quantified data can often take too long for rapid TLC loops, or require more analysis to be useful than it is possible to perform in the time available. IT can improve the availability and usability of information where it is needed, as both George Day (1999, pp. 101-122)[2] and Stephan Haeckel (1999)[3] advocate; however, lower tech solutions can be very helpful. For example, at Tesco they held monthly cross-functional meetings explicitly devoted to experiments and small-scale innovation. Tesco had these once a month. The Strategic Marketing Director ensured that this meeting had timely and relevant information.

- **Orientation** through Situation Awareness is the centerpiece of rapid TLC loops. It is based on the development of intuition through experience as well as a good insight into the general market environment. This in turn requires deep expertise in the key players. Therefore the most experienced and skillful marketers should drive this part of the process, integrating the various strands of information and activity into a coherent whole. It is also greatly aided by the development of rules of thumb - what works around here - to capture knowledge and enable the organization to retain as much of this intuitive understanding as possible (See Chapter 6).

- **Decision-making** is not the keystone of the regular TLC process - orientation is. However, as described in Chapter 6, rigorous challenge by a senior manager outside the regular process is necessary to help the marketers sustain Situation Awareness. When and how this challenge is initiated becomes a critical factor for success. In most organizations it fits into the business calendar in quarterly or annual planning reviews. This is probably sufficient in most cases. However, in more volatile times some form of early warning system is needed to help companies sense market problems that would in turn lead to ad hoc challenge outside the normal time table.

- **Action** requires the greatest integration between functions inside and outside of marketing. A common problem is that marketing information and actions are siloed from execution functions. This slows down TLC loops, creating the dreaded "treacle" effect, where everyone seems to be plowing through a viscous liquid, struggling to get things to happen in functions that are still trying to follow earlier direction based on information that is increasingly out of date. Since the "Commit" stage of TLC needs to continue the rapid pace of Test & Learn, the Commercial Operating System has to reach into the other operational functions and not just marketing and sales.

However, as well as ensuring that the process has been developed for Agile Marketing, it also needs to coexist with the rigorous ADAM processes. There is a natural tension between the discipline to follow standardized processes and the intuition required for fast TLC loops.

One solution might be for the TLC and ADAM processes to be driven by different people. However, integration is more straightforward if the same person leads both the fast-loop process and the rigorous approach. This may seem a stretch, but I believe it is analogous to the "helicopter" ability often looked for in top management (i.e., the ability to see things from a very high level and then zoom in to the detail as well). In many commercial areas of business, my observation is that the best managers are able to act intuitively precisely because they have mastered the basic processes. An analogy can be found in sport. In sports where "seeing the field" to react to the opponents' moves is critical, such as soccer, rugby, American football, or tennis, the best players are so strong technically that they can be confident in their execution of even the most difficult moves and thus able to react instinctively. In other words, the more expert and capable your marketers are, the less serious the tension is. As they develop their intuition they have less need to go through the formal processes step by step.[4]

An example of this loose/tight approach is in retailing. Buyers always have some limitations on how much of the company's resources they can commit in the form of what is known as the "Open-to-Buy" process. This is a tool that is normally in place for fashion and seasonal merchandise, providing a budget and planning tool to manage commitment and investment in stock. But the best buyers know when and how to push the boundaries of the rules for particularly good deals. By balancing the intuitive feel with the financial discipline these top performers could maintain control while being more agile. A buyer who could not use the Open-to-Buy process and simply overbought would be dangerous to the financial stability of the business; a buyer who followed the rules but had no feel would not risk early bankruptcy, but would lose share and be equally dangerous to the long-term future.

Combining these elements of the OODA loop with more traditional processes in this way provides the best opportunities to enable rapid experimentation.

SKILLS AND PEOPLE – INTUITION THROUGH APPRENTICESHIP

The last example illustrates the fact that in order to succeed in executing the processes, the successful Commercial Operating System depends on having the right people with the right skills in the positions that drive performance.

I pointed out earlier that there is some consensus on the types of organizational capabilities that are required for market orientation. People need to be good at market sensing, market responding and creating customer relationships, while in addition I have argued that they need to execute smart experimentation and fast-loop response, based on a combination of facts and intuition.

In Chapter 6, I argued that the key to speeding up the action/decision loops of marketing is to develop better intuition in front-line marketers through developing their Situation Awareness. This in turn implied that developing the necessary capabilities depends on two forms of experience.

First, marketers need to be immersed in the customer experience of the product or category so that they can develop an intuitive understanding of the customer. Second, they need to know the specific landscape in which they are competing, through experience in selecting fit offers within the business and marketplace context.

These two sources of experience enable marketers to develop the right mental models not only of the customer but also of how their own business and other market participants (suppliers, distributors and competitors) may react. Indeed, since intuition is developed in a particular company situation it can be very risky simply to assume that lessons and rules of thumb learned in one market can transfer to another.

To summarize the implications for people and skills of the previous chapters, marketing people need to be seasoned in their marketplace and have developed the necessary intuition; they need to be able to understand and use market research; and they need to empathize with their customers. They also need to have an action orientation. Integrators need to be good at strategic thinking, leading and motivating teams, with sufficient analytical horsepower to make sense of the many different sources of information they receive about both the marketplace and their own internal costs. Specialists need to be expert in their chosen field and be able to communicate their insights to the broader marketing teams.

Unfortunately, this wish list does not match the majority of marketers. My experience is that even where they are customer oriented, most marketers lack the skills to operate in a fast-loop marketing approach, in particular intuitive expertise in customer behavior combined with analytical horsepower and an action orientation. Of course this is not true of all marketers; indeed, an objection that has been raised to this argument by colleagues who are strategists rather than marketers, is that they consider it obvious that marketers should have relevant experience, and find it hard to believe that this is often not the case. How can this situation have arisen? I would point to four primary causes.

First, I believe that this is in large part because a myth has grown up in the marketing community that if you can market one thing, you can market anything. Thus any job search results in numerous applications from marketers who have moved from industry to industry. This results in marketers with generalist rather than industry specific skills, meaning a risk of poor Situation Awareness in a particular marketplace.

This in turn is because marketing has sought to portray itself as a profession, with agreed tools and techniques to "do marketing". In a search for the "rules of marketing" the belief has grown that if you have the techniques and experience in using them, you can market anything. (The only real counterexample is probably between B2C and B2B marketers, where there is limited crossover.) I have heard this described as "physics envy" – the idea that like physics, we should be able to do the same thing anywhere in the word and obtain the same results. It implies that technique can replace intuition, which is disproved by the work of Klein and others. Technique can certainly enable intuition, hence the need to develop the tools of the trade, but intuition is the desired goal.

This is exacerbated by the common phenomenon of marketers changing job frequently, either within their own company between products or between companies. The result is that they build limited insight into customers while the employer loses what understanding they have gained.

A second problem is that marketers have been taught to believe that the route to greater success is in general management. They therefore are continually looking for ways to escape their current role and function, in direct opposition to what is required for real success. P&G under AG Lafley identified this problem and sought to reduce the amount of churn. It downplayed the idea that marketing was a stepping-stone to general management and upgraded the importance of the role in the business.

In contrast to the first two problems, which result in inexperienced marketers, the third problem is that marketers have traditionally undergone very little formal training to develop the techniques. They therefore lack the skills to interpret or act on the information in the marketplace. These marketers rely overly on intuition in the absence of the tools and techniques that could help educate it. Consequently, their intuition is based not on a full experience of the marketplace but on limited data. There are marketing qualifications, but only a tiny percentage of marketers have them. (Arguably, this is because of the belief that technique is not the key, intuition is. Of course I agree with this. But I also believe that technique is a great enabler of developing intuition. As with many professions, being able to do the right things well allows you to focus on the softer, more important issues that lead to better mental models, stronger intuition, and more rapid and accurate execution.)

The fourth problem is that some marketing people are simply the wrong people to recruit into an Agile Marketing organization. They lack the basic intellectual skills to work in the ways I have outlined for evolutionary marketing. Entering a discipline that shouts about its intuitive approach to big leaps – the Steve Jobs approach – these are the marketers who value creativity over commerciality. Many of them are not numerate. This means they will neither be looking to win scarce resource in the marketing landscape, nor taking full account of the true situation reported to them by the facts. No amount of training will help these individuals succeed as Agile Marketers.

Of course, one solution to having the wrong marketers is to recruit different ones. For example, Capital One copied its recruiting approach from management consulting firms. When looking for marketers, it sought smart people with an analytical orientation and the potential to be great business leaders. From my own experience, the need to recruit new marketers is often underestimated. There is little more dispiriting than investing in a large training program for marketers who lack the intrinsic capabilities to perform the roles they are being asked to. Their presence slows down the training program and they typically leave for an easier life soon after anyway, wasting all the investment of the employer.

Historically, to solve the problems many employers recruited marketers who had gone through the great fmcg marketing academies such as P&G, Unilever, Mars and Coca-Cola. They hoped that these recruits would know all there was to know about marketing and could bring their magic to new employers. But of course, this falls foul of the first problem – they may have the right expertise, but they have the wrong experience.

So some new recruits are probably needed, but unless recruited from a very similar company, they will still need to develop the necessary intuition, while those who are not new recruits will probably require training in the new processes discussed in the previous section.

The large marketing capability building programs of recent years have partially addressed this problem by providing "in-house" training for marketers. For example, Diageo insisted that every marketer be trained in DWBB, putting 6000 of them through a tailor-made program in four years, and also insisted that all senior marketers should lead training two weeks per year. This training has the advantage of being tailored to Diageo's own marketing landscapes. Training is also performed through the burgeoning number of tailored training programs at business schools, as well as the advent of Corporate Universities. Each of these allows tailoring to the relevant markets.

Unfortunately, in some respects these large programs, designed to train marketers in Big Leap marketing, may on their own have made the situation worse. This is because, even if the program is well tailored to the Commercial Operating System of the employer, in emphasizing rigorous processes, frameworks and tools, the training detracts from the critical importance of intuition and Situation Awareness. Graduates of these programs will still lack depth of experience in the specific market to develop the necessary intuitive competence.

In order to develop the critical skills, therefore, formal training is necessary but not sufficient. It needs to be complemented by real world experience. Formal training can teach the main elements of the Commercial Operating System and the tools and processes. In addition, however, I propose that junior marketers need to be "apprenticed" to more senior experts.

The apprenticeship model has been developed over centuries as the best way to transfer knowledge from a master to an apprentice while enabling the apprentice to develop his own intuitive competence, his own creativity and ultimately his own approach. Apprenticeship is far more than teaching. According to Wikipedia,[5] apprenticeship is a system for training a new generation of practitioners of a skill. A master craftsman was entitled to employ young people as an inexpensive form of labor in exchange for providing formal training in the craft. Most apprentices aspired to becoming master craftsmen themselves on completion of their contract (usually a term of seven years), but some would spend time as a journeyman and a significant proportion would never acquire their own workshop.

Today, the apprenticeship model is alive and well in many countries, not just in the traditional trades, but also in professional services such as law and accountancy, where the newcomers to a firm are assigned to one or several more experienced colleagues (ideally partners) and learn their skills on the job. One of the most important aspects of apprenticeship is that the apprentices are given the freedom to express themselves rather than becoming a clone of the original master. In this way trades, professions, and, I believe, marketing can advance.

In marketing there are formal ways to encourage this when kick-starting a training program or a transformation, e.g., by appointing mentors to the people running the tests. However, more important are the informal ways in which a senior marketing manager engages with the more junior marketers to articulate the intuition she is using when testing, learning and comitting. She can also provide them with the opportunity to conduct their own TLC marketing while the senior manager provides the rigorous challenge.

To summarize, the skills of your marketers are critical to executing the processes of Agile Marketing. In particular, they need to be seasoned marketers in your markets with intuitive insight into the marketplace, analytical capabilities to absorb information and an action orientation. They will not be "generalist marketers", but numerate experts in the marketplaces in which they compete. This will require an apprenticeship model to be developed and nurtured amongst the marketing community, supplemented by formal training where appropriate. Finally, over time these skills need constant updating, not least as new frameworks and tools are introduced.

FRAMEWORKS AND TOOLS – FEW AND HELPFUL

Managers are clear about the need for frameworks and tools for increasing the speed of obtaining customer feedback and incorporating it into business response: "We spent three months unable to respond to the changes in competitor and supplier strategies because our systems neither picked up the changes nor allowed us to change prices quickly enough, which cost us millions of Euros in profit" (European MD, Industrial Components manufacturer).

In some respects improved frameworks and tools are the easiest part of a Commercial Operating System to develop. Nobody needs to lose power and there is no threat to your job. However, this apparent simplicity often hides the fact that most marketers either reject the new tools or can't use them. Worse, the supposed ease of application often means that people think new frameworks and tools are the entire answer: "We will fix marketing by putting in place a new CRM system." The most visible outputs from a marketing capability-building program are the unused manuals on the shelves full of new tools to be used in various commercial processes. So the question is how to introduce the frameworks and tools successfully.

Experience suggests two requirements for successful introductions. First, ensure that each one is truly focused on improving performance, limiting the number of frameworks and tools that are brought in. Second, engage the marketers in the development and adaptation of the tools, rather than impose them from above.

In Chapter 8, I identified new market research tools that can help develop insights into customers and the fitness landscape and thereby improve the selection of the fittest variants. This typically means replacing existing approaches such as focus groups and Usage and Attitude surveys with tools more focused on behavior: a mix of qualitative research, quantitative research and advanced econometrics.

These techniques are well known to the research community, yet rarely used in important marketing decisions. This is in part because market research has a history of not being targeted on specific marketing goals. When they are, the results can be powerful. The British pub and brewing company, Greene King, did not have a history of using market research, but when it faced a market upheaval in the pub industry, it developed a small number of hypotheses of ways it might respond to the customer and competitive changes. By using these hypotheses to drive its market research, and conducting conjoint analysis combined with observational qualitative research, it was able to identify promising courses of action to experiment, far more quickly and valuably than by simply researching the historic market dynamics. The research tools were successfully adopted because they helped marketers improve their offers, rather than simply providing data.

Similarly, IT often seems to result in information overload for marketers rather than helping to improve the offer. CRM systems in particular often create more confusion than insight. This is not, however, a justification for ignoring the potential of IT in marketing. In the proliferating complexity of the marketing landscape, intuitive marketers need all the help they can get to develop their Situation Awareness.

In fact, the concept of Situation Awareness, as originally developed by Mica Endsley,[6] is focused on designing computer systems, and in particular user interfaces. Although Endsley's work is largely in high speed, mission-critical operational contexts such as nuclear power station control systems or aircraft systems, the same principles apply to marketing systems. IT should be used to filter information to decision makers in a way that enhances their Situation Awareness. One pitfall to avoid is removing information that might help them understand the context of what they are seeing. The key is to help marketers develop the right mental models, to avoid the blinkered vision of attention tunneling, to reduce the load on the marketer's memory, and to provide appropriate warning signals of things that may be going awry.

I pointed out earlier that Tesco Clubcard data analysis is focused on answering decision makers' issues, taking care to avoid overload, in contrast to Safeway's ABC Card analysis, which overloaded the marketers. The best CRM systems help marketers understand their market environment and make it easier to experiment, rather than either confusing them with too much information or over-automating activities so that marketers lose awareness of what is happening.

Another example is a problem that businesses face in an increasingly global business environment. Performance across countries, customers and products is often hard to track rapidly enough to drive decisions when they could be most useful.

Alfa-Laval, a Swedish based engineering company, found that while its accounting and operational systems contained all the information to assess what had happened with prices in the past, it was inadequate to support a new, more agile pricing strategy. By breaking down the pricing challenge into strategic pricing issues and operational pricing issues, it was able to develop two relatively simple, PC-based decision tools. The first of these helped Alfa-Laval improve its fitness and speed of response to commodity price changes in adjusting its list prices (a strategic pricing issue) while the second ensured that price and discount decisions with individual customers took full account of all relevant factors.

Together these tools and the consequent effort to build overall pricing capability were anticipated to improve return on sales by over 3 percentage points (a 30% profit improvement). As with all IT, the simple but powerful lesson is that that you need to work out what specifically you are trying to use it for.

In the case of Alfa-Laval, the new tools and processes were rolled out gradually through the group, engaging the marketers and sales forces in how to introduce and adapt them to different local markets. This helped to overcome any instinctive resistance from intuitive marketers to imposed templates and processes.

Similarly Microsoft, a company that historically resisted systematization and rigid processes, introduced a new marketing spend framework to improve efficiency across its European region. By using a bottom up approach based on pilots and workshops tailored to each country, it was able to build a new capability with strong buy-in from its marketers.

In summary, frameworks and tools are a critical element of an agile Commercial Operating System. On their own they can achieve little. But when used to improve processes and build skills, with due attention to real marketing issues and the development of Situation Awareness, they provide a stepping stone for the Company Way of Marketing.

METRICS AND PERFORMANCE MANAGEMENT – CUSTOMER FOCUSED, THOUGHTFUL ABOUT FAILURES

It is an old adage that what gets measured gets done, but nonetheless true for that. The final element of the Commercial Operating

System addresses the challenge of supporting the other elements with appropriate metrics.

The first measure that needs to be defined is "fitness". This is of course the basis of the evolutionary approach. For some industries, such as retailing, defining fitness is relatively straightforward. I have argued that it is behavioral, and is typically best measured by share of customer spend.

However I have also pointed out that other stakeholders' views may be very important and need to be combined with the customer perspective. For other industries, the challenge is greater. For example, where the company has a very low share of a large market, share of spend may not give a useful picture. Here revenue may be a good proxy, but revenues may prove to be very volatile, which makes reading the results of experiments very tricky. In these cases an Evolutionary Marketer may be forced into using measures that are less directly behavioral. If so, there is an even greater emphasis on the intuitive feel for the market.

Once fitness is understood, there are most likely some obvious changes that need to be made, usually resulting from performance management systems that have not kept pace with the change to customer centricity.

One of the most frequent barriers quoted by executives who have tried to improve the market orientation of their company is that the performance management system got in the way. "Our customer services managers were so focused on operational performance that they measured how quickly a customer's call was answered and handled but not how satisfied they were afterwards" (Brand Manager of UK consumer services group).

These executives found that they needed to realign their performance targets and incentives to match the desired customer focus. It is a common challenge that performance targets are not driven by customer measures: "Our product development has been so focused on patenting new innovations, which was their primary performance target, that they are now three years behind the market leaders on launching the products that our customers are already asking for" (Business Unit Head of global chemicals company).

Another common problem they found was that salesmen who were incentivised on sales volume did not follow new rules on prioritizing profitable customers or only doing what is right for the customer, if the salesmen believed that it would cost them money. Here the performance management had to be adjusted to reward, respectively, margin and customer satisfaction.

Performance management systems can also struggle when there is a rapid movement of personnel, since that limits accountability for longer-term growth and profitability. This has been seen most recently in the banking sector where bonuses have been paid for performance that was, in retrospect, a mirage. One response to that is to delay the cashing out of any reward. For example, European financial regulators now demand that bankers, whose bonuses had depended on annual performance alone, will now be paid according to a system that tracks performance and the bank's share price over a three-year period, with only a small proportion paid out as cash. A similar scheme could be put in place in other industries, delaying bonuses to marketing and sales until the full results of their efforts can be observed.

But beyond making these obvious changes, a couple of more subtle pitfalls await the unwary.

First there is a risk both of having objectives that are either too broad or too narrow. For example, Knudsen et al. (2006)[7] recount the story of a beverage company that made both mistakes simultaneously. The accountability of brand managers was too narrow, focused only on brand equity, while account managers had too broad a metric: volume. The company improved its Commercial Operating System by adapting these metrics, emphasizing brand gross margin contribution in brand management performance, and providing greater granularity to its key account managers by including profitability as well as cost, time and quality targets.

Second, there is the danger, discussed in Chapter 8, of market research and metrics that are focused on image and abstract "needs" rather than behavior leading to sales and profit. In order to ensure its experiments targeted real behavior, Capital One's Information Based

System focused on behavior rather than attitude. It looked short term at customer response, but the accounts that responded were also "incubated" over a longer period to see whether the credit risk (which as the credit crisis shows, can be critical) was acceptable.

The previous examples apply to most businesses trying to become more customer-centric. However, my recommendations to institute fast experimentation create some new challenges. For example, Thomke (2006, p. 208)[8] reports that the door development team at BMW in the 1990's was rewarded for providing nearly perfect data on the crashworthiness of a door, which took months to generate. Yet the computer simulation approach for crash testing required rough data much earlier. So management needed to adapt the performance management system to reward speed rather than accuracy.

Similarly, the difference between failures in experimentation and mistakes needs to be accounted for. Since evolution involves much failure, the metrics need to allow for it. It is often described as "encouraging failure". But equally the aim is to encourage successful adaptation over unsuccessful adaptation. After all, any fool can keep on failing. There needs to be a short time frame during which failure is acceptable, but a longer one over which it is not – a time frame that is, of course, adapted to the environment in which the business competes. However, even then, it does not necessarily mean the individual has failed – rather the opportunity is not available. At 3M, a skunk works team chasing after a new idea is not fired if the idea flops - the failure is marked up to experience and the team members move on.

In addition, repeated mistakes due to carelessness or poor management are rarely a valuable contributor to learning. There is a difference between a poorly designed experiment that results in unusable information and a well-designed experiment that does not work but which provides valuable learning. The critical difference is whether the individual and the business is learning from the failures, or repeating the mistakes. Of course, distinguishing between the two is very difficult, but a manager with a holistic understanding of her direct reports ought to be able to do so over time.

It may seem that the biggest obstacle to adopting TLC is the high failure rate of variants, which is integral to the approach. This apparently goes right against the grain of someone brought up on management approaches that are supposed to succeed every time. However, the nature of Evolutionary Marketing does not in fact imply constant failure. Its essence is to keep the current fittest offer until it is beaten by a new variant, so at all times the marketers should in fact be successful overall, and moreover improving continuously. So the traditional manager needs only to tolerate constant experimentation, not constant failure.

Nevertheless, a few tips are in order to help TLC marketers identify appropriate metrics and performance management approaches.

1. Keep track of what experiments are being tried out and why. This will help assess whether an experiment was designed properly and to capture the learning. (Of course this should not be a bureaucratic process – weekly team meetings may be sufficient to discuss this.)
2. Be vigilant to winnow out the unfit marketing offers, and keep track that this is really happening. This is the core of natural selection, without which costs will escalate and unfit offers proliferate.
3. Measure and reward the execution of committing. As a step that goes well beyond marketing, its success needs to be part of the performance measures of all involved in the integrated system.

Finally metrics and performance measurement may provide tension between TLC and ADAM. Just because TLC loops are tolerant of offers that prove to be unfit, does not mean that a rigorous ADAM process should be. If ADAM is being deployed, this should be because management believed that it would be useful – in particular that the future could be sufficiently well predicted to support a planning approach. So here, performance management should be cognizant of the distinction and far less tolerant of failure.

∽✺∾

Successful Agile Marketing businesses have different capabilities from more traditional Big Leap or Attritional Marketers. In addition to a focus on the customer, they emphasize speed and they focus on the few core processes that will make a real difference to their performance. This in turn means they need a coherent Commercial Operating System (COS), with well-aligned processes, skills, frameworks and tools, and performance management system.

Structure, Culture and Commercial Operating System form a potent combination; but what should a marketer do, who is reading this and thinking that I am not describing her company? What are the early steps required to transform it into an Agile Marketer?

NOTES

1   Knudsen, T.R., Moret, C. & Van Metre, E. S. (2006). The power of a Commercial Operating System. In Webb, (Ed.) *Profiting from Proliferation* pp. 61-71. New York: McKinsey & Company.

2   Day, G. S. (1999). *The Market Driven Organization.* New York: Free Press.

3   Haeckel, S. (1999). *Adaptive Enterprise.* Boston: HBS Press.

4   For those who dislike sporting analogies, another is the field of mathematics. Most people think of mathematics as the ultimate analytical discipline. But in fact the best mathematicians are highly intuitive pattern-finders. They must be able to check their intuition through rigorous analysis, and technical excellence is a vital tool, but few would expect to discover new results purely through analysis.

5   Wikipedia. *Apprenticeship.* Retrieved November 30, 2010: http://en.wikipedia.org/wiki/Apprenticeship

6   Endsley, M. R., Bolté B., and Jones, D. G. (2003). *Designing for Situation Awareness*. New York: Taylor & Francis.

7   Knudsen et al. (2006). The power of a Commercial Operating System, p. 67.

8   Thomke, S. H. (2003). *Experimentation Matters*. Boston: HBS Press.

CHAPTER 15

GETTING STARTED

By now, I hope that you are convinced that a more agile, adaptive and intuitive approach to marketing can result in better offers, faster and more cheaply. So if you want to become an Agile Marketer, how do you get started?

In this chapter, I will suggest a practical way to address the major challenges to becoming more agile that are noted throughout the book. You may not be surprised to learn that my suggestion for getting started is a fast experimental loop. I have argued throughout that marketers can usually find their way better in a competitive market environment by adopting a fast Test-and-Learn process than by extensive planning. As you will see, you can also use fast TLC loops to develop an Agile Marketing process that works for you.

In a recent HBR article, Thomas Davenport outlined an experimentation process.[1] This proposed a very analytical version. I have adjusted the model (Figure 15-1) to reflect the idea of testing intuitively against mental models discussed in Chapter 7.

How to conduct Agile Marketing: Test, Learn, Commit (TLC) loops

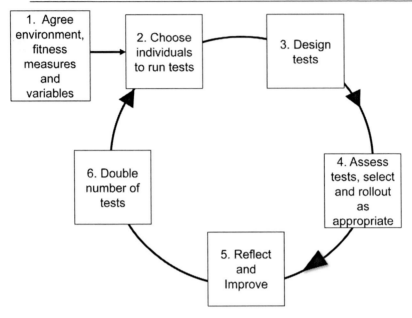

Figure 15-1

The key to the learning loop for becoming an evolutionary marketer is to start testing in a small way and then to increase the pace and degree of testing.

A typical marketer does a lot of thinking and carries out a small number of tests en route to a big leap. He might, for example, consider two product variants, three packaging variations, two price points, and four possible ad campaigns, and do pre test market simulations on these, followed by an extended in market test of two combinations, before committing to a major launch of one of these.

The Evolutionary Marketer, on the other hand, will carry out hundreds of different tests in market, and research thousands in simulations. This is possible in part because each of the elements of the marketing offer can be tested, so that trying out 5 variations on each of 5 possible variables results in over 3000 variations.[2]

To move from one camp to the other, the key is simply to start doing more tests. So my recommended approach is as follows:

1. Agree what environment you are competing in, what fitness measure you will use and which parts of the marketing offer you can vary. As with any process, it is important to have clear objectives – what will success look like – before starting. By agreeing this, the marketing team can reorient itself away from traditional image and attitudinal measures towards simple behavioral measures.

The principles of Agile Marketing are firmly grounded in the Darwinian theories of Evolution and of Natural Selection. In biology, the environment in which a creature competes may seem to be fairly obvious, certainly to the creature itself. However, in fact the entire ecosystem may impact on the creature's fitness. Similarly in marketing it is important to be clear about the environment in which you are competing. Which customers are you trying to attract, what competitors are there already?

Equally in biology the goals are clear: survival and reproduction. You will need to find their equivalent in your market. What metrics best define fitness? In chapter 4, I argued that gaining share of customer spend was the primary metric in many cases. But a new Agile Marketer will need to agree which customers and which spend. Furthermore, the response of other stakeholders may be of more or less importance. Can the share of spend be achieved at acceptable levels of profitability; is there any reason that employee response to the offer will be damagingly negative?

It should come as no surprise that managing to the wrong metrics could throw the entire endeavor of Agile Marketing off-course. Equally, it needs to be recognized that, just as the entire ecosystem in biology is hard to discern at first glance, so the true market environment may not be obvious from the start. In other words, the definition of the environment and of fitness should each develop over time, just as the marketing offer does itself.

The best measure is market share for most markets. If you need something more complex, including e.g. risk measures as with credit cards, then so be it. But keeping it simple is best.

2. Choose the right people to run the test. The key to fast loops is having people who can use their intuition to skip over the decide phase directly into action. As we saw earlier, intuition is best developed through Situation Awareness (SA). SA means a marketer has an intimate knowledge of his customer and competitive environment. He is able to process market information rapidly and thereby assess the fitness of his market offer at any time. SA is in turn developed on the job through experience (which as pointed out earlier, implies that marketers cannot easily switch industries). So the people who run the test should be immersed in the market and sufficiently analytical to examine the facts rather than be driven by their biases.

The problem that the leader of a business seeking to develop Agile Marketing skills may face is that none of the current marketers have good Situational Awareness. With marketing people moving from industry to industry they lack the time to develop the necessary experience and mental models. Or she may have people with the necessary intuition, but who are unable to adapt themselves to the new approaches of Agile Marketing.

Furthermore, the essence of Agile Marketing is "test and learn". Learning requires a combination of paying attention to the facts and using these facts both to select winners and losers and to refine your own mental models. Some supposedly intuitive "gut instinct" marketers may not, in fact, have good intuition to develop marketing offers in their competitive environment. They may be applying inappropriate mental models.

In Chapter 13, I argued that apprenticeship is the way to develop more junior marketers into experienced TLC marketers. But when you have not operated with fast TLC loops in the past, you may not have the people to play the role of master to these apprentices. The challenge is to choose people to start this process with the intrinsic capabilities who will learn on the job but without the opportunity to be apprenticed to experts.

You should look for open-minded thinkers able to balance analysis and intuition. They will rapidly build their experience and intuition through the tests.

3. Run the first tests. With the right people in place, the TLC process needs to be kicked off with one, simple, test. Superficially, running the first few tests should be straightforward, since every organization will have run some sorts of marketing trials before. However, getting started in any new endeavor is never as easy as it seems.

The nature of those prior trials may be completely different from what is now required. The difference lies in the amount of random variation allowed in a test versus the amount of thoughtful "tinkering", to use the term introduced in Chapter 4. Most marketers are used to running tests to prove they are right. A few are used to running a small number of tests to find out which of two or three alternatives is best – e.g., for price or advertising weights. But in each of these cases the thinking effort is done in advance and once the test has been run the marketer commits to the result and moves on to another issue. If all the tests fail, then the marketer has failed. So experiments are typically slow to be started, run for a long time, and the results used to make a Big Leap decision.

The mind-set required for TLC loops is completely different. There are many more tests to be run, while the result of the first test is simply a starting point for the next one. There is always the opportunity to adapt further to the ever-changing environment. So in reality, it does not really matter if the first test experiment is an abject failure, you just try some more.

The challenge, then, is to get started on tests and to build momentum in evolving new marketing offers, rather than using the trial to obtain a once and for all answer to a question.

My advice would be to start with pretty much any test and get used to going rapidly round the TLC loop.

4. Measure the test results, learn and commit as appropriate. Following the Test, Learn, Commit approach, the next step is to find out whether the tested offer was better than the initial offer, and if so to select and commit resources to it. If not, of course, then the initial offer remains the best.

Just as the mind-set required when undertaking a test is likely to be completely different from what the marketing department is used to, so is the mind-set for learning. Marketers need to discern which tested variation was fittest, using the metrics chosen in Step 1, and rapidly choose which directions of variation to drop and which to pursue. This is in contrast to the usual approach to learning, which would be to find explanations for the results, developing new theories if there were surprises.

New evolutions of the more successful experiments need to be tested in the marketplace as soon as possible. This will mean far less post mortem analysis and more "just doing it."

The challenge is simultaneously to keep adding new experiments while building marketers' intuition and Situation Awareness rather than getting stuck in analyzing old experiments. This does not imply zero analysis or thought. However, the emphasis should be on selecting a new test and thus building up direct experience, more than continuing to focus on analysis of the first test.

5. Reflect and improve. After this initial test, there is the opportunity to reflect on what was learnt and then to improve the marketing offer where the test demonstrated greater fitness.

When reflecting, there are two sorts of learning to consider:

- *Learning about the market offer.* Which one was better, were we surprised, was there any detail about the result that can point new directions for the future? Can we begin to develop rules of thumb?
- *Learning about the testing process.* Did it go as we expected – both in the market and within our organization? How can we improve it going forward – speeding up or reducing the cost of trial, improving the measurement approach, managing internal processes to act and select rapidly? Did we use facts sufficiently or were initial biases dominant?

Regarding improvements, it might seem obvious that when a successful experiment has been identified the organization will commit to it. However that fails to take into account two realities about organizations. First, somebody always seems to continue to believe in the losers, and thus wants to divert some resource to developing them. Second, commitment requires action from people who were not involved in the experiments.

The first issue may be less of a problem with Agile Marketing than with traditional marketing, since the sheer number of experiments should mean that each individual experiment would have less invested in it, both in terms of resources and psychologically. However if someone is convinced that exploring a particular part of the fitness landscape will be fruitful but the results do not support him, the problem remains.

Similarly, the willingness to commit your resources to somebody else's new idea, even if backed up by experimental evidence, may be made easier if there is a continual stream of such new initiatives – but not if the overall philosophy of Agile Marketing is not yet well accepted beyond the marketing department.

Both these problems have their roots in the organizational and cultural challenges of Chapters 13 and 14. Over time, people will build trust in the new approach and develop unity, while structural changes can ensure responsibilities are crystal clear. But initially, the business leadership will need to pay special attention to ensuring that successful tests are followed through – that there is real commitment to them.

6. Double the number of tests. Easy to write: hard to execute. Having gone round the loop once, go round the loop again, doubling the number of tests each time. If you double the number of tests you run every cycle, then the total number you run a year will grow rapidly. If a testing cycle lasts 3 months, say, you could be running over ten thousand tests in your fourth year.

TEST, LEARN, COMMIT TO THE APPROACH

Throughout this book I have resisted describing exactly what an organization should do to implement Agile Marketing. This is because I believe that each business should execute the approach in its own way. Just as marketing offers should be adapted to their environment, so should marketing processes. What works for one company in one industry may be very different from what works for a different situation.

In fact, since the challenge is to find a process adapted to your environment, the approach in the previous section uses TLC loops to develop the skills of Agile Marketing. Start with one or more initial approaches, learn from the successes and failures, and commit to what works. Then experiment further with adaptations of the process.

The successful Agile Marketer will have become used to working in a fast-loop way by rapidly increasing the amount of testing and learning she does. She will have good Situation Awareness of the "marketing process environment". Unfortunately an organization that is just starting out will lack that Situation Awareness and will probably feel uncomfortable at the early stages of the process. But the key is to persevere: to test, learn and commit to ever improving iterations and within a year a robust approach will have been developed.

At some point, possibly quite early, but possibly later than you think, the number of tests will become overwhelming for the organization. This is the point at which the organizational issues will need to be addressed. For many businesses this will be challenging. There may be a temptation to stop at the number of tests you can manage easily – perhaps supported by calculations of how expensive it will be to continue multiplying the number of tests. However, I expect that by this stage there will already be major and surprising successes for the agile approach – offers that have done much better than expected, or competitors who have been unable to respond to your actions, or surprising insights that have led to real innovation. This may provide the platform for more lasting organizational change and more tests than you originally thought possible.

That's it! There is no point in my going into greater depth on the challenges of getting started, because the whole point of being agile and adapting to the environment is that the specific steps are different in every situation.

In this chapter I have laid out the challenges of implementing Agile Marketing and proposed an approach with a few steps that anyone can take to get started.

The main steps are:
1. Identify the market environment and key metrics
2. Choose the right people
3. Run the first tests
4. Measure the test results, learn and commit to winners
5. Reflect and improve on both the offer and the process
6. Double the number of tests.

It is not simple to go from a few tests designed to confirm what marketing already thinks to thousands of tests designed to explore the market environment. But as Tesco, Capital One and the other cases discussed in this book demonstrate, the upside is enormous. It is surely worth starting on the journey. Good luck!

NOTES

1   Davenport, T. H. (2009). How to Design Smart Experiments. *Harvard Business Review, 87* (February), 68-74.

2   Mathematically, this is 5 to the power of 5, which is 3125.

INDEX

Lightning Source UK Ltd.
Milton Keynes UK
173768UK00002B/2/P